MAKING PILLOWS

OVER 30 PROJECTS FOR
MAKING & DECORATING CUSHIONS

MAKING PILLOWS

OVER 30 PROJECTS FOR MAKING & DECORATING CUSHIONS

Linda Barker

Photography by Lizzie Orme

a Salamander book

A SALAMANDER BOOK

Published by Salamander Books Ltd,
129-137 York Way,
London N7 9LG,
United Kingdom

Distributed by
Random House Value Publishing, Inc.
40 Engelhard Avenue,
Avenel,
New Jersey 07001

A CIP catalog record for this book is available from the
Library of Congress.

ISBN 0-517-14092-6

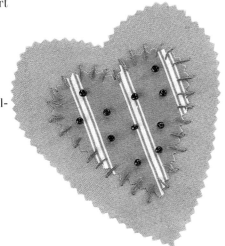

CREDITS
Author: Linda Barker
Project manager: Jane Donovan
Editor: Emma Callery
Design: Watermark Communications
Photographer: Lizzie Orme
Stylist: Linda Barker
Illustrations: Terry Evans
Film: Creative Text Ltd
Color separation: P&W Graphics
Printed and bound in Great Britain

Contents

Introduction

Pillows are one of the easiest accessories to make for a room. They can add an essential finishing touch to the decor and they can be used in any room of the house. Pillows instantly add vitality, pattern and texture, and give a splash of color to a sofa, chair or bed. Or use them to soften hard seating or to pad the arms of an old armchair. In a living room, for example, a sofa piled high with piped and tasseled pillows makes an inviting focal point and irresistible resting place. Pillows for your head, feet, even the small of your back, make reclining an art form. Who could resist such comfort? A chair placed near a window, softened with feather pillows and cushions, persuades you to come and sit down, relax, and stay a while. Or a bright frog-shaped beanbag cushion on the nursery floor invites a small child to jump all over it.

Make pillow covers from fabric remnants and trimmings found in flea markets or antique sales. Whatever catches your eye, gather it up and store it away - you never know when it may come in handy. In this book, the pearly buttons I found in a thrift store are used to decorate my lacy buttoned covers (see page 75) and are so much prettier displayed around the edge of a pillow cover than hidden away in a cupboard.

Only a couple of facts remain consistent throughout the book. First, all the fabrics you choose to use should be colorfast and preshrunk to avoid shrieks of horror when a floor cushion comes out of a washing machine with a marbled-effect design! Second, check that fabrics can be easily cleaned. A "dry clean only" fabric may look wonderful, but it is going to cost a small fortune in cleaning bills every time a sticky-fingered child chooses to use a treasured pillow cover as a hat, or as a container for candy or peanut butter sandwiches.

With these exceptions, there are no hard and fast rules for choosing the right fabrics for pillows and cushions. For example, it is possible to use dress fabrics as well as heavy upholstery fabrics with equal success. Search out scraps of inexpensive fabrics for sewing appliqué panels and patchwork, or look for remnants of rich, extravagant fabrics with the knowledge that just half a yard isn't going to break the bank. In some of the projects that follow, I have displayed a piece of lace on a pretty gingham ruffled cover, sewn scraps of fabrics to make charming appliqué designs and traditional patchwork, and even transformed a shrunken old sweater that may otherwise have been thrown away. I hope to encourage you to do the same.

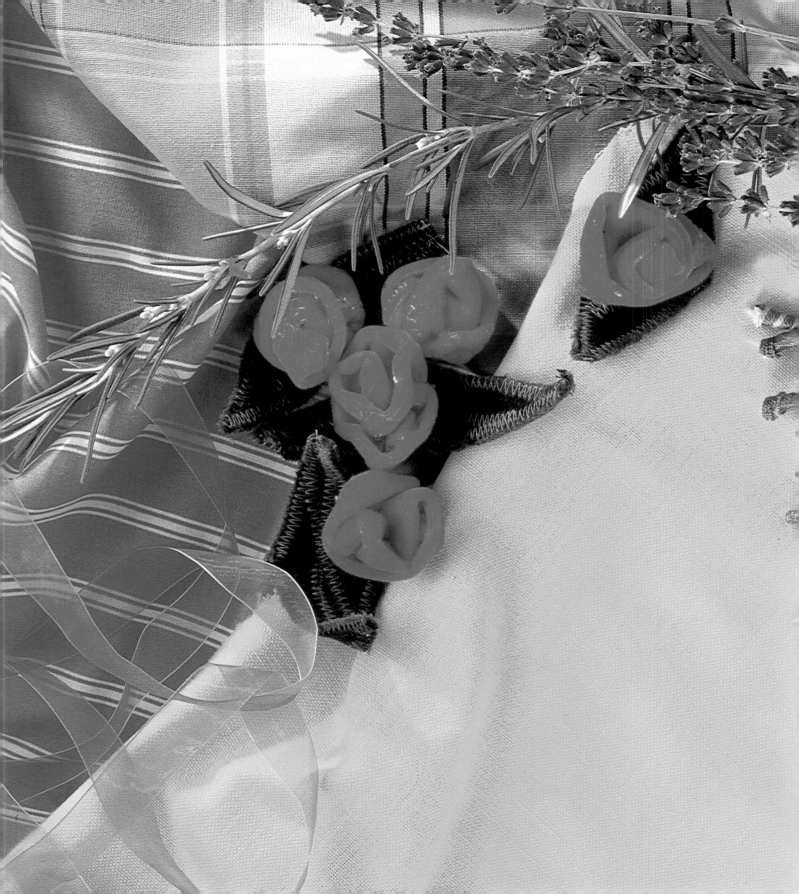

Materials and techniques

Before tackling any of the pillows in this book, it is well worth looking through this section as there are many techniques described that will make your pillow-making so much more straightforward. In this way, the end result will be even more professional.

MATERIALS

A basic sewing kit should provide you with all the equipment you will need for the projects in this book. I keep all my bits and pieces together in a plastic tool box, which has handy compartments for pins, tape measures and thread. I keep the following items in my sewing kit at all times:

Good scissors Both a larger pair for cutting out and a small embroidery pair of scissors are indispensable for pillow-making. Pinking shears are useful, too, and may be a worthwhile investment if you intend to do lots of soft furnishings.

Tailor's chalk A supply of this for marking out fabric is preferable to pencil marks, and it is easily removed.

Cloth tape and retractable steel tape measures These are inexpensive items of equipment that I wouldn't be without.

Graph paper Needed for most patchwork designs.

Steel dressmaking pins These will not mark the fabric or leave holes. Occasionally, I use longer glass-headed pins, particularly for holding thicker fabrics together, such as for quilting and appliqué.

Needles It is worth having these in assorted sizes, as well as darning needles and bodkins for threading work. Variously-sized sewing machine needles are also necessary so you can alter them according to the weight of fabric being sewn.

Thread My supply increases after each job because I am reluctant to discard even the smallest amount left on a reel. Generally, you should always use a thread that is compatible with the fabric you are working on. Strong threads for heavy canvas and denim-type fabric; lighter threads for gauze, organdy and silk. Choose natural threads for natural fabrics and, likewise, synthetic threads for synthetic fabrics.

Zippers These should be of the correct weight and size for the cover fabric. Usually a 10 inch zipper will be sufficient to allow most sizes of pillow forms into a cover, but smaller or larger ones can be used according to the size of pillow. I almost never use a metal zipper, as they do not wash as well as the plastic ones, nor are they as discreet.

Miscellaneous items Other useful things to keep at hand are packs of neutral-colored bias binding tape, batting and self-covered buttons of all sizes. A particularly well-used item in my sewing kit is a plastic seam ripper, designed for quickly unpicking stitches.

GLOSSARY OF FABRICS

This list includes all the fabrics I have used in this book, and a few that I have not used, but I feel would be suitable. Remember, that by adding unusual bits and pieces you personalize your covers, setting them apart from any others you may buy in a store.

Batting A soft and fibrous cotton or polyester padding which is available in several weights. It is used for quilting.

Burlap A very strong, coarse-weave fabric made from jute or hemp.

Canvas (also referred to as heavy cotton duck) A strong fabric, sometimes woven from linen and occasionally from synthetic fibers. It comes in a variety of weights: lightweight is the most suitable for pillow-making.

Chintz A cotton fabric that is either printed or plain and has a characteristic glaze finish.

Damask A self-patterned traditional fabric made from cotton, linen or silk on a traditional jacquard loom. It is often used for tablecloths and napkins.

Denim Characteristically used for blue jeans, but can be purchased off-the-roll for upholstery and covers.

Felt A fabric made from matted fibers that are pounded, shrunk and bonded together to make a soft fabric that does not fray when cut.

Gauze or lightweight muslin A very soft, light fabric, woven quite loosely, making it semi-transparent.

Gingham A traditionally woven, checked fabric. Usually cotton or mixed cotton and synthetic fibers.

Lace A delicate, fine, open-weave fabric created by knotting or twisting the threads to form a pattern. It is usually white or cream.

Linen A strong cloth woven from flax fibers. It is prone to shrinkage and creasing if it is not mixed with another fiber.

Muslin lining or heavyweight muslin A woven cotton fabric, lighter than canvas. It is usually sold in its natural colorway, but it may be bleached white or dyed.

Organdy A finely woven, thin fabric that is semi-transparent and stiff.

Plaid A traditionally woven fabric in two or more colors creating a checked cloth. Individual designs relate to specific Scottish families or clans.

Provençal print A traditional French country print fabric with brightly-colored, small-scale motifs and floral patterns.

Raw silk (sometimes known as wild silk) A natural fiber that is spun and then woven into soft fabric with a slubby, coarse texture.

Silk dupion A slubby, textured silk, but is now often made from other fibers.

Tapestry A heavy, woven fabric, often showing a traditional pictorial design.

Ticking A heavy cotton, twill fabric used for pillows, mattresses and bolsters. Traditionally woven with a fine stripe in black, blue or red.

Toile de Jouy A traditional cotton print in one color (usually red, blue or sepia) on a natural or off-white ground. The designs often depict rural scenes and rustic figures.

Velvet A soft, luxurious warp pile fabric with a dense, short pile.

Using the templates at the back of the book

On pages 90-94 are a series of templates designed to be used with the pillows in this book. Either photocopy them as they are or enlarge to an appropriate size and then cut out the template.

If you do not have a photocopier to hand, trace the designs and transfer onto paper by drawing over the back of the tracing with a soft pencil and then going over the front again; or enlarge them using the grid method. To do this, draw a grid of squares over the relevant template in the book and draw a correspondingly larger grid on your sheet of paper. Copying the outline square by square, reproduce the design.

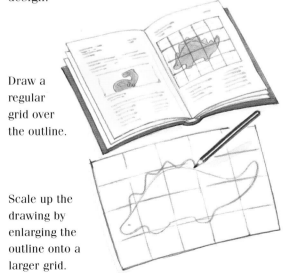

Draw a regular grid over the outline.

Scale up the drawing by enlarging the outline onto a larger grid.

CLOSINGS

Whether your pillow is closed with a zipper or an envelope fastening, or a simple tied fastening, always decide on the method of closing before purchasing or cutting out the fabric. Each closing will require a different amount of fabric. If you are in any doubt, cut the pillow pieces from paper before you begin and lay these onto a flat surface to determine the amount of fabric you will need.

Occasionally the best option for closing a pillow is to simply stitch the opening closed. For the projects in this book where I feel this is necessary, I have included this process in the relevant text.

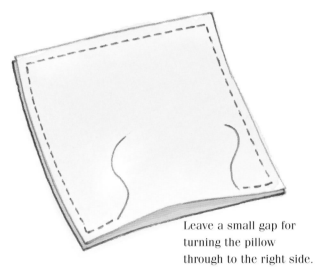

Leave a small gap for turning the pillow through to the right side.

ENVELOPE CASING

This is perhaps the simplest fastening. Cut the required square of rectangle for the front of the pillow cover, including a 1 inch seam allowance. Cut out a second piece for the back of the cover, the width of which is the same as the first piece, but the length should be one-and-three-quarters the length of the front. Cut this piece in half across its length. Turn the raw edges under along each side of the horizontal cut.

Lay these two pieces over the pillow front, with right sides together and raw edges even. Stitch around the sides and turn the cover to the right sides through the opening.

For a button-backed closing, sew buttonholes and buttons onto the two parts of the vent prior to stitching the front to the back.

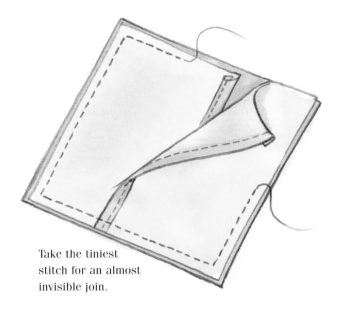

Take the tiniest stitch for an almost invisible join.

INSERTING A ZIPPER

There are two options for inserting a zipper. The first is to insert it along the outside seam, and the second to insert it across the center back of the pillow. With the exception of shaped pillows the choice is yours. Here it is recommended that you insert a zipper across the center of the back to avoid fitting a zipper around curves, which can look bulk and untidy.

Fitting a zipper in the seam Cut the front and back parts of the cover, including the seam allowances. Place these with right sides facing and keeping the raw edges even. Place the zipper centrally along the edge of the seam and mark the ends of the zipper using chalk.

Sew the ends of the seam up to the chalk marks. Then baste the seam where the zipper is to be stitched. Press the seam open and lay the zipper wrong side up, along the basted seam. Sew it into place using the zipper foot on your sewing machine. Undo the basting and open the zipper. Stitch around the other edges, keeping the right sides of the fabric together and the raw edges even. Turn the cover to the right side, through the zipper.

Fitting a zipper across the back of the fabric Cut the front of the pillow cover as before, and cut another piece to the same size plus a further 2 inches to the width. Fold this piece of fabric in half and cut across the center. Lay these two halves together with right sides facing and raw edges even, and mark the central position of the zipper using tailor's chalk. Continue as for fitting a zipper in the seam (above), first sewing the ends of the seam up to the chalk marks.

TIED CLOSINGS

Another closing option is to fasten a pillow with fabric or ribbon ties. The simplest way to do this is to leave one side unstitched and then sew the ties on the front and back. On larger pillows it is advisable to include a flap inside the closing edge to stop the pillow pushing out around the ties (rather like a pillowcase flap). To do this, make the front slightly longer than the back. Seam one of the short edges and fold to the back until the length of the front is the same as the back. Stitch front to back with right sides facing, as usual.

Alternatively, ties can be sewn at both sides of the envelope casing (see above) on the reverse of the pillow, to be tied neatly at the back.

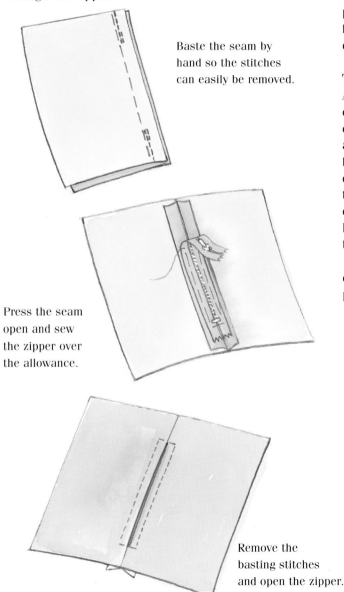

Baste the seam by hand so the stitches can easily be removed.

Press the seam open and sew the zipper over the allowance.

Remove the basting stitches and open the zipper.

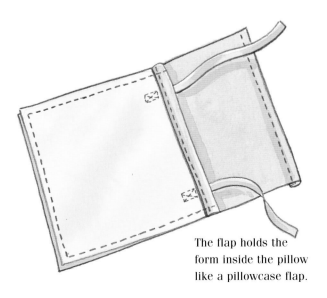

The flap holds the form inside the pillow like a pillowcase flap.

MAKING SHAPED PILLOWS

Shapes and sizes of pillows are limitless, ranging from tiny rectangles that support your neck to huge floor cushions that may provide an answer to a seating problem. Square, round, hexagonal, even star-shaped - the choice is up to you. Armed with a paper template, you could make just about any shape of pillow or chair cushion you could imagine.

SHAPING TO FIT A CHAIR SEAT

To shape a cover to fit a chair seat, simply lay a sheet of brown paper or newspaper over the seat and mark around the perimeter with a pencil. Cut out the template and fold it in half to check that it is symmetrical, and then lay this onto your fabric and pin in place. The best filling for this type of squab cushion is foam, providing a flattish cushion with a firm support.

Lay the paper directly onto the seat and draw the outline.

If you're making a squab cushion or a closed fastening, cut the shape from a double layer of fabric.

MAKING A HEART-SHAPED COVER

First fold a sheet of brown paper or newspaper in half, and then draw half of a heart shape onto the paper, or use one of the heart-shaped templates on page 90. Use the foldline as the center of the heart and cut it out from the double thickness of paper. Unfold to reveal the whole, perfectly symmetrical, heart-shaped template. Pin this directly onto your fabric and cut out the front and back of the pillow, bearing in mind which type of closing you need (see pages 12-13). If you want to put a zipper into the middle of the back, see page 36 for cutting and sewing.

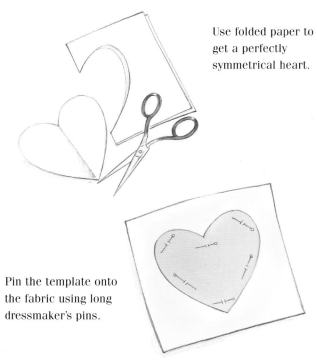

Use folded paper to get a perfectly symmetrical heart.

Pin the template onto the fabric using long dressmaker's pins.

MORE COMPLICATED SHAPES OF PILLOW COVERS

For a shaped pillow that is more complicated in design, such as the daisy-shaped cushion on page 36, break down the separate components used to make up the design. In this case, the seat cushion is simply a round center and you can use a dinner plate to make the circular outline. For the petal template, the base of a glass tumbler is ideal, but remember to extend both lines from the edges of the glass downwards to square the ends of the petals prior to sewing.

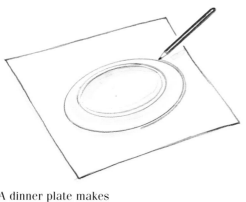

A dinner plate makes an ideal guide to draw around.

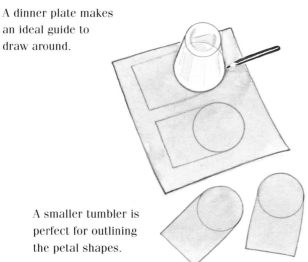

A smaller tumbler is perfect for outlining the petal shapes.

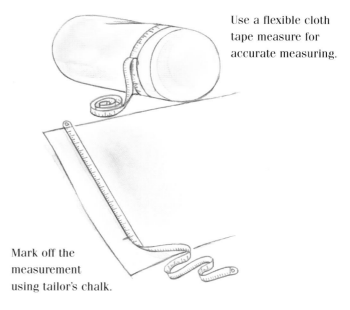

Use a flexible cloth tape measure for accurate measuring.

Mark off the measurement using tailor's chalk.

PILLOW FORMS AND FILLINGS

Use a pillow form with either a feather or a down filling, or one with a mixture of both. Nonallergic cotton and polyester fillings are also suitable. Plastic or latex foam chips are less expensive, but these tend to compact and become lumpy after a time and need to be replaced.

Some of the pillows in this book are filled with foam cut to size with a pair of sharp scissors. For deeper pillows, such as the damask piped squab on page 49, either fill with a deep piece of foam, or insert two thinner layers.

Always use fillings and pillow forms with the relevant safety standards. This information is always supplied with those products that have been fully approved.

MEASURING A BOLSTER PILLOW FORM

Bolster pillow covers are shaped to cover the size of the pillow form. For a bolster that has both ends gathered, you need to cut a rectangle of your chosen fabric, the width of which is equal to the circumference of the bolster plus a 2 inch seam allowance. The length needs to be the same as the bolster, plus the radius of each end and a 1 inch seam allowance for each end.

MAKING YOUR OWN PILLOW FORM

For shaped pillows you will often have to make your own pillow forms. Use the same template as for the pillow and cut two pieces of gauze or muslin to a size slightly larger all around. With right sides facing, sew the front and back together, leaving a small gap. Turn the right sides out, stuff with loose filling, and sew the gap closed. Use this as a form for the pillow.

EDGINGS AND TRIMS

Decorative edgings and trims can make all the difference to a pillow, and there are many types to choose from. Ready-made trims are easily available and can either be stitched around the edge of an existing pillow cover or sewn between the top and bottom pieces of a new cover. Whichever method you choose, they are quite straightforward to apply.

SEWING ON TRIMS

Measure all around the edge of the pillow cover and add on an extra 2 inches to the measurement for joining. Hand-sew the trim to the edge of the cover, using strong thread and tiny stitches. Make a small hole in the seam with a seam ripper and tuck the ends of the trim inside the pillow cover.

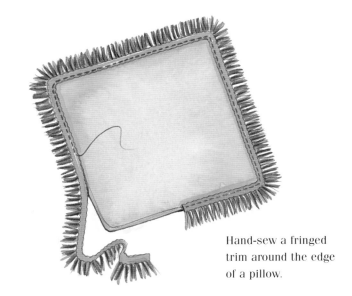

Hand-sew a fringed trim around the edge of a pillow.

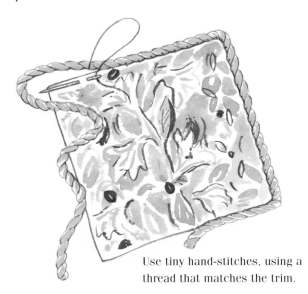

Use tiny hand-stitches, using a thread that matches the trim.

ATTACHING DECORATIVE CORDS

To stitch on a decorative cord, use a strong thread in a complementary color and use tiny stitches to sew this along the edges of the cover. To join the cord, unravel the ends slightly and then twist the cords together. Oversew the ends to neaten and prevent the threads from unraveling around the cord.

STITCHING TRIMS AND RUFFLES

Lay the trim or ruffle along the edge of the right side of the top of the pillow cover with the fringe or ruffle toward the center of the pillow. Align the heading tape or fabric edge with the raw edge of the pillow. Pin the trim and then stitch around the four sides, keeping an even seam allowance.

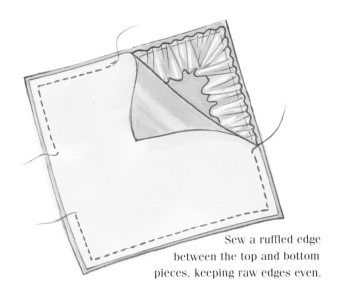

Sew a ruffled edge between the top and bottom pieces, keeping raw edges even.

PIPING

If you have difficulty finding a trim to match your pillow, make your own corded piping. Mark out 2-inch-wide strips across the diagonal (bias) of your fabric, using tailor's chalk and a long tape measure. Cut the resulting strips from the fabric.

Open up the small seam and press.

Cut the bias strips across the grain of fabric.

Join the strips together across the grain, pinning the strips together with right sides facing and at right angles to each other. Sew together, trim, and then press the seam open at the back. Fold the bias strip around the piping cord, with the right side uppermost and aligning the raw edges. Use the zipper foot on your sewing machine to stitch as close to the edge of the cord as possible. Always use the zipper foot because this will allow you to stitch close to the cord. If the regular sewing foot is used, you may find that the casing fabric will start to pucker.

Pin the piping along the edges of the right side of the top of the pillow cover, keeping the raw edges even. To fit it around the pillow corners, snip into the piping's seam allowance. Pin and then stitch in place.

To join the corded piping, do not sew the two ends onto the fabric. Instead, unpick the stitches from one end of the piping and fold the fabric back. Cut the cords to butt up together and fold the fabric back over the cord. Fold under the raw edge and enclose the piping. Hand-sew in place.

SAFETY NOTE

Care should be taken when sewing on trimmings, beads and buttons, because you might find that babies and small children could pull these off if they are not very firmly stitched in place.

If you are making pillows for the nursery or for very small children and babies, it is best to avoid making pillows that are decorated in this way.

Care should also be given when purchasing pillow forms and fillings, making sure these are protected with the appropriate safety standards.

EMBROIDERY STITCHES

Often a little hand-stitching is used to embellish the detailing on the front of a pillow cover. Also, occasionally, hand-stitches are better than those produced on the sewing machine for performing certain tasks, such as a double line of running stitches for gathering long ruffles.

RUNNING STITCH

Small neat stitches of equal length are stitched on the front and back of the fabric. When stitching a line of basting, if inserting a zipper for example, use this stitch, but with longer stitches on the right side and smaller ones behind. Use a contrasting thread which is easily seen for removal once the main stitching is finished.

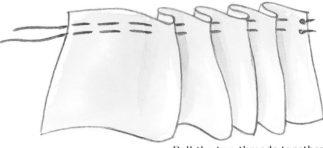

Pull the two threads together to gather up the fabric.

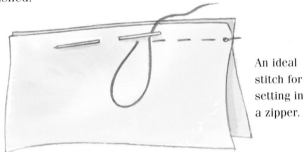

An ideal stitch for setting in a zipper.

DOUBLE RUNNING STITCH

Work evenly-spaced stitches across two rows, a short distance apart. Leave the threads loose at one end and slide the fabric along the threads, gathering the folds evenly. Tie off the loose ends.

BACKSTITCH

This is a short stitch which is strong enough to hold seams if necessary. Sew one stitch and come through the top fabric with the needle as if to start another stitch. Take the needle backwards and insert it at the end of the previous stitch, bringing the needle back up an equal stitch length in front. Repeat to finish a line of stitches. Three backstitches sewn on top of each other are often used to tie-off threads.

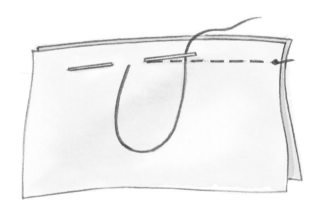

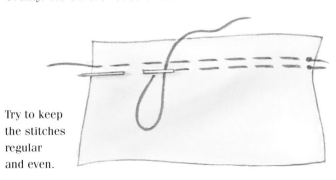

Try to keep the stitches regular and even.

Vary the lengths of the stitches depending on the look you want, but keep their length even.

LADDER STITCH

Use this stitch when sewing appliqué designs onto the right side of fabric, where a neat, discreet stitch is needed. An oversized version of this is used in a decorative way around the canvas panel on the stenciled pig pillow (see page 81).

Working on the right side of the fabric, knot the thread and insert the needle from the back to the right side. Take a stitch exactly opposite the point where the needle has come out, pass the needle underneath, and then bring it out as before, only a little further along the seam. Progress as before.

For a line of invisible stitches, use a thread that matches the face of the fabric. However, sometimes - as in appliqué - you may wish to sew an overstated stitch, in which case you should use three strands of a colored embroidery thread and a larger stitch. Regardless of the length of the stitch, always keep the stitches even and follow a regular spacing between each stitch.

CROSS-STITCH

Use three strands of embroidery thread to sew this stitch. Knot the thread and bring the needle up from underneath the work. Stitch down into the diagonal corner, bringing the needle down through the work and then upwards to a point directly opposite where the needle had first come out. Move the needle across to the opposite diagonal and through to the underside, creating the characteristic cross.

Repeat the procedure to complete the stitches, remembering that half stitches may be formed around the outside of a shape if required.

This extremely popular and easy-to-execute stitch is elegant when used as decorative detailing on the cover of a pillow. Use a classic combination, such as blue on white fabric, for an attractive finish.

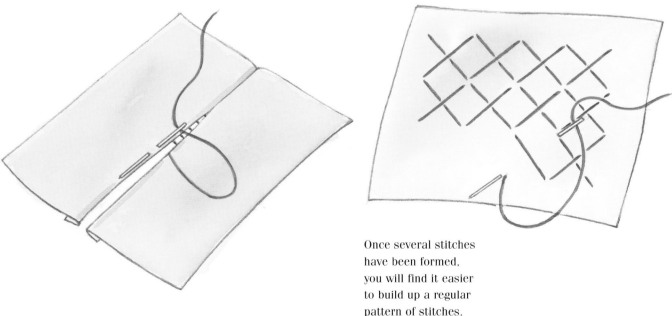

Use tiny stitches for an invisible seam.

Once several stitches have been formed, you will find it easier to build up a regular pattern of stitches.

QUILTING

Quilting has traditional roots and yet its application can be both modern and traditional. The technique outlined here is stitched on a sewing machine and is simpler in comparison to the hand-quilted fabrics so often seen in museums and magazines, and it takes up only a fraction of the time to produce.

1 Place a layer of batting between two fabric pieces to create a sandwich effect with the main fabric uppermost. Baste around the edges and pin across the center with long, glass-headed pins.

2 If your main fabric has an outline to follow, such as the fruit and flower urn on the pillow on page 27, then follow this with the line of stitches.

3 When you are machine-quilting, it is easier to work the lines of stitching between an embroidery hoop, as this keeps the fabric taut at all times. Work from the middle of the work out. In order to slide the double hoop underneath the sewing foot you may need to remove part of the foot, but once the hoop is in place fit the foot back onto the sewing machine. Remove the pins from the area to be quilted within the hoop.

4 Drop the feeder teeth on the sewing machine so you can guide the fabric underneath the sewing foot wherever you wish to go. Twists and turns in the direction of sewing are easier to do when the teeth are retracted.

5 To establish the flow of stitches, and because there are no teeth to pull the fabric through, move the embroidery hoop to feed the fabric under the sewing foot. It may take a little while to get used to this technique at first, but keep practising and you will get there. It is best to work on a piece of scrap fabric before committing to the real thing. Follow the outline printed on the fabric and feed the fabric under the needle, as if you were drawing with the needle.

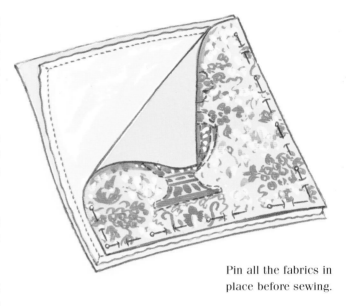

Pin all the fabrics in place before sewing.

6 Once enough of the design has been stitched, remove the hoops and the remaining pins (if there are any) and neaten the work. There will be many small threads to snip off and the fabric can then be used to make up a pillow cover.

If you start to use the sewing machine continuously, say for four or five minutes at any one time, you will need to rest the motor. Do this by stopping sewing for approximately two minutes for every five minutes sewing on the machine.

Quilting can also be sewn with straight lines in the more traditional manner of squares or diamonds. If you wish, you could use this more regular form of machine-quilting as an introduction to the freestyle method of quilting.

If you use the ready-quilted batting, you will already have a regular grid which will form a guide for your stitch lines. Pin the top fabric underneath the batting with long dressmaker's pins, and then carefully sew over the stitching lines. Turn the fabric over to reveal the right side.

APPLIQUÉ

One of the delights about working in appliqué is that all the materials are found in bags of scrap fabrics and that basically you are stitching something from practically nothing at all. With a small piece of fabric here, and a larger piece there, you can easily create great images.

1 Separate your fabrics into patterns and plains, textures and colors. Some fabrics are easier to work with than others. For example, velvet will fray until it disintegrates into practically nothing, whereas felt does not fray at all and because of this quality it is perfect for appliqué. That is not to say that I never use velvet for this type of sewing - the combination of many fabrics makes for an interesting match.

2 If using fabrics that are susceptible to fraying, if at all possible oversew the raw edges with a sewing machine using a zigzag stitch (see the appliqué hearts pillow on page 34). However, some pieces will be so small that this is not possible and, in the end, it is best to avoid using these.

3 Once you have decided upon your design and which fabrics are going where, cut out the individual pieces, remembering to add a small allowance all around for turning under. Carefully press under the turnings and stitch in place.

4 Arrange the fabric pieces on the background cloth, pin, and then sew in place, using tiny, invisible stitches. Turn under raw edges wherever possible to avoid the fabric fraying.

5 Embroidery stitches can then be applied over the appliqué, adding decorative detailing. Experiment with different stitches as you go along, filling in parts of the design or simply adding small details. Beads and sequins can also add to the overall effect of the appliqué. Sew these decorations on very securely, using a strong thread.

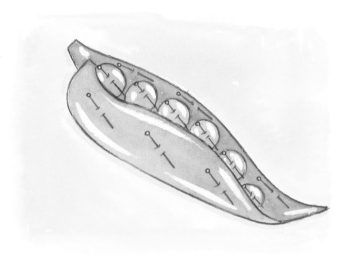

A peapod is a very simple outline for appliqué.

Appliqué can be inspired by many things, even something as simple and commonplace as this peapod, or the carrot that appears on page 38. It may be that you have a particularly beautiful piece of fabric that inspires the design, or something you have seen in a store, museum or gallery.

Books and magazines can be equally wonderful sources for reference. If you do not have the space to store old magazines, then tear out pages that interest you and keep these together in a large manila envelope or two. It is amazing how looking back through these old collections of images can often spark off new and innovative ideas.

Also get into the habit of saving every scrap of fabric - tiny scraps can be stored in jelly jars, and larger pieces neatly placed into bags or shoe boxes. Sort the fabrics by color and if the collections become too big, then sort them out yet further, this time by texture and pattern.

PATCHWORK

Patchwork must be one of the oldest country crafts and whereas a quilt can sometimes take years to complete, a patchwork pillow will only take up a fraction of that time.

1 Work out your design on a piece of graph paper. You could use a traditional design, like the Ohio star used for the patchwork pillow on page 51, or make up your own design. Whichever you choose, draw it carefully onto the graph paper.

2 Cut the pieces from the paper using a pair of sharp scissors, following the lines diligently. To help with your piecing later on, mark which shapes join together on the back of each piece of paper.

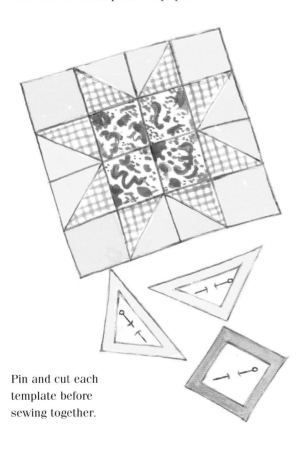

Pin and cut each template before sewing together.

3 To make stronger templates, use stiff cardboard instead of graph paper and use the resulting shapes as master templates. This is particularly useful if the same shape is to be used again and again. Place the cardboard templates on scrap paper and draw around them to make as many paper shapes as are required, and then cut them out.

4 Choose a selection of fabrics that work well together. Plain fabrics will offset patterned ones, and dark colors will project paler ones. By assembling the groups of fabrics, you will be able to assess what each of them will do.

5 Pin the templates onto the wrong side of the fabrics and cut out each piece, adding a small seam allowance on each side. Turn the allowance over to the back of the template and baste. Continue this until all the templates have been basted.

6 Stitch together the patchwork pieces. Start in the center of each design and work your way outwards. To stitch pieces together, place with right sides facing and hand-sew the two parts together, using tiny overstitches. Continue to make up the patchwork in this way. Do not remove the paper until each square, or part of a design, is complete.

7 The patchwork pillow featured on page 51 uses four such stars. Should you become addicted to the whole process, continue making the Ohio stars until the patchwork becomes a bedspread.

8 If the process is becoming labored, then sew two stars and two plain squares together - positioning them diagonally - to make up the front of the pillow cover. Or easier still, sew one single Ohio star for the center of the pillow and then border this with plain fabric pieces. With ideas like this, you will find that it is very easy to adapt the patchwork to suit your own special requirements.

STENCILING

Stenciling is addictive - so be warned. The little pig featured on the stenciled pillow on page 81 will be almost guaranteed to turn up on bedroom walls, pillowcases, quilt covers, and the rest. But who could resist it?

Cutting stencils is easy once you have the right equipment to hand. A sharp craft knife, some stencil card and a cutting surface is all you require.

1 Either use the pig outline on page 90 or design your own stencil and draw the outline onto the stencil card.

2 Tape the card to the cutting surface and cut out the outline using the sharp craft knife. Always cut away from your supporting hand and turn the cutting surface as you move around corners.

3 Attach the stencil to the surface to be decorated with double-sided adhesive tape.

4 Use fabric paint and stencil the design by dipping a slightly damp stencil brush into the paint. Dab off the excess onto a piece of scrap paper or paper towel, and transfer the paint through the stencil. Use a tapping motion with the brush.

5 In larger areas, vary the pressure used on the brush to provide lighter and darker shaded patches. This will give more interest to the overall design.

6 Leave the fabric paint to dry thoroughly and set the paint according to the manufacturer's instructions. Usually it is set with a hot iron smoothed over the reverse side of the fabric.

7 Remove the stencil and position elsewhere if repeating it for another pillow. Check the back of the stencil before repositioning to make sure no paint has dripped onto the reverse of the design.

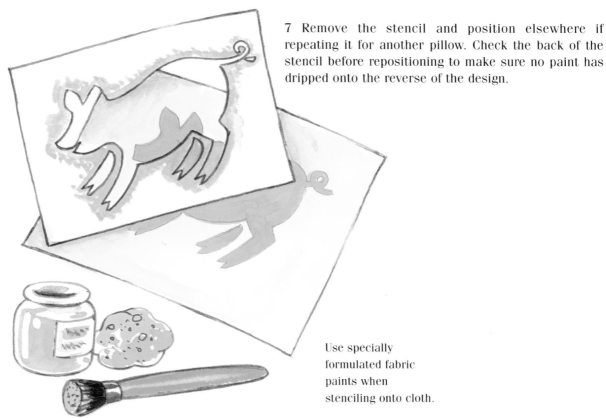

Use specially formulated fabric paints when stenciling onto cloth.

Stitched pillows

This chapter will show you how to use a few basic stitches to add character to your pillows. If you're looking for inspiration or you simply need a cover to copy, then flick through the pages to see which pillow would suit your interior.

Quilted pillow

Most fabrics are suitable for quilting, but a material with a pattern, such as this flower and fruit urn, provides a really obvious outline to follow when stitching. So this type of fabric may be the best kind to look out for if you are quilting for the first time. The quilted appearance occurs because of the layer of batting sandwiched between the face and base fabrics. As the line of stitches progresses around the outline, the quilting becomes more noticeable. This method of quilting is done on the sewing machine (see page 20), but traditionally quilting was done by hand and involved many hours of dedication and diligence.

Cut the face fabric to the required size and place this over a similarly-sized piece of batting, which in turn is placed over a cotton backing cloth. Use long pins to secure the three layers together and then machine-quilt the design on the fabric, as outlined on page 20. Follow the outlines of the printed design and aim to keep the stitches as regular and as even as possible.

As one area is stitched, release the embroidery hoop and pull an unworked area through the hoop. Remove the pins from this area, squeeze the hoops together, and continue as before. Carefully work as little or as much of the design as you wish, continuously checking the effect as you progress.

Cut the fabric pieces for the back of the pillow, taking into account your preferred method of closing (see pages 12-13). Then sew the front and back parts of the pillow together, with right sides facing and raw edges even. Turn the right sides out and insert an appropriate pillow form (see page 15).

If you prefer to do some freestyle quilting, sandwich a layer of batting between two pieces of plain fabric and pin them together as above. Then lightly draw your design onto the fabric with tailor's chalk and follow these lines when stitching. Look at antique quilts in museums or contemporary pictures in books to find inspiration.

Left Place the face fabric over the batting, which in turn is placed over the base fabric. Use long pins to hold together.

Right Sew around the outlines of the printed motif, stitching as little or as much of the design as you wish.

Beaded heart pillow

For this pillow, stitch two fringed pieces of canvas diagonally opposite each other on the front of the pillow cover and decorate the other corners with pretty muslin hearts that are first crossed with thin ribbon and then decorated with tiny beads.

Natural colors are very restful, and here I have used toning lining-weight muslin and canvas in addition to the natural cotton ribbon. As both the fringed canvas and the beaded hearts are stitched onto the top of the pillow, first prepare the cover. Cut the fabric pieces for the front and back of the pillow, taking into account your preferred method of closing (see pages 12-13). Set the back fabric aside.

Fold the front into quarters and press lightly with a warm iron to mark them clearly. Cut two pieces of canvas to fit neatly into two diagonally opposite corners and carefully cut these to exactly this size, less 1 inch all around.

Fringe the four edges of each piece of canvas by teasing out the fibers to create a 1 inch fringe. Pin and then sew each piece of canvas onto the cover, keeping the stitching line close to the inside edge of the fringing.

Enlarge the larger heart template on page 90 on a photocopier to an appropriate size or transfer it onto paper (see page 11). Use the template to cut out two muslin hearts, and then cut strips of thin cotton ribbon to make a checkerboard pattern over the surface of the heart. Pin the ends of the ribbon in place to hold them prior to sewing.

Once the ribbons are stitched, trim them up to the edge of the hearts and then pin each heart in place on the front of the cover. Use a close zigzag stitch on your sewing machine to sew around the outside edge. Finally, sew each tiny bead onto the heart at the points where the ribbons cross.

Sew the front and back parts of the pillow together, with right sides facing and raw edges even. Turn the cover to the right sides and insert an appropriate pillow form (see page 15).

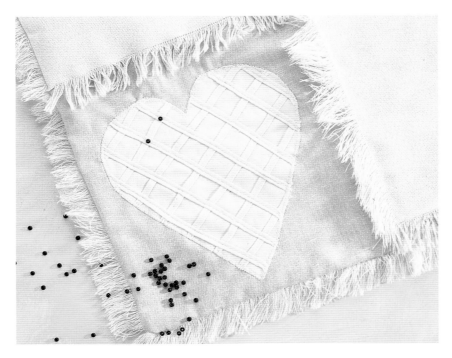

Left Small beads are used for practical reasons more than any other; it would be uncomfortable to rest your head against beads that are any larger than these.

Right The natural colors of this pillow emphasize the beadwork.

Blue cross-stitch bolster

Bolster pillows are extremely comfortable for supporting the neck, either on a bed or on a sofa. The ends of this pillow are simply gathered and trimmed with a ribbon, stitched neatly over the gathering stitches. As an alternative, cover a large button with the same fabric as used for the blue and white fabric trim and stitch these over the ends.

Cut a rectangle from an appropriate fabric, following the measurement instructions given on page 15. Sew three evenly spaced, 1-inch-wide strips of blue and white fabric across the rectangle to run around the bolster. To cover the raw edges, sew a strip of lace over each edge. If your lace has a line of threads forming a channel, such as the one I have used here, thread a narrow ribbon through the threads and tie with a small bow at the front for pretty detailing.

Sew the long ends of the bolster together, aligning the lace strips and with right sides facing and raw edges even. Press the seam allowance open and turn to the right sides. Turn under the seam allowance at each end and stitch, and then run a line of gathering stitches close to the machine-stitching, using a strong thread.

Slide the bolster pillow form inside the cover, leaving an equal amount of fabric at either end. Pull up the gathering threads at each end and stitch these closed to fasten the ends of the bolster. Tie with a decorative ribbon if required, or stitch on a pretty covered button over the gathers.

Draw a heart and a diamond shape onto the front of the bolster in the gaps between the three strips, and work cross-stitch into these shapes (see page 19). If your bolster cover fabric does not have a square weave to follow, it may be easier to cross-stitch the heart and diamond motifs onto a piece of Aida canvas (specifically made for embroidery work), as this will produce an even cross-stitch pattern which can be sewn directly onto the pillow cover.

Right Perfect for supporting the head, this bolster pillow would be just right on a sofa or bed.

Embroidery squares

For this pillow, tiny squares of translucent organza are stitched over silk flower petals. Each square is then decoratively stitched using pale embroidery thread, resulting in a delicate pattern that is strikingly beautiful. I chose a loose-weave burlap fabric for the background, as its rough texture contrasts perfectly with the fine organza.

Cut a burlap square to the required size of the finished pillow, plus 1 inch all around for turnings. Press the fabric carefully, taking care not to twist the weave in any direction. Lay the fabric on a flat surface and smooth down.

Strip a silk flower head for its petals, making sure all the plastic parts are removed from the flowers. Press each flower carefully using a warm iron and a damp cloth. Position the flowers over the surface of the burlap following a regular pattern (see below), but do not pin them yet.

Cut 2-inch squares from the organza using pinking shears. If you do not have these, brush a little white glue around the cut edges of each small square to prevent the edges fraying.

Place each organza square directly over each flower head. Holding the center lightly with a finger, with your other hand move the flowers slightly from underneath the organza so some of the petals project beyond the edges. Vary the extent of the projection for each flower and from which side of the square they project. Pin the squares and silk flowers onto the burlap.

To create the hand-stitched spiral coils, use two strands of embroidery thread and a simple backstitch. Lightly draw the coils with a piece of tailor's chalk before stitching. Make sure that some of the stitches trap the petals underneath to secure the flowers to the burlap fabric.

Once the decoration is stitched, iron the fabric once again. Select a straight stitch on your sewing machine and sew around the edges of each organza square to keep the squares flat and prevent fraying. Stitch the burlap over a cotton fabric and trim to the same size. Then stitch this and a backing fabric together, taking into account your preferred method of closing (see pages 12-13). Finally, insert an appropriate pillow form (see page 15).

Left Once the position of the silk flowers is determined, pin each organza square onto the burlap.

Right The delicate flowers and translucent organza are perfect contrasts against the burlap weave. This pillow measures 17 inches square, but you could make one to suit your own requirements.

Appliqué hearts pillow

Each square on this attractive pillow has been decorated with a heart motif, using scraps of different fabrics. Each square of linen with its appliqué heart is then embellished with colorful embroidery thread and tiny beads. The effect is wonderful, and yet it is gloriously easy to do.

The beauty of this technique is that you can use many different textures and colors of fabric, which all combine to create a rich effect. Choose from inexpensive gingham and felt, linen and printed cotton, as well as more luxurious velvet and silks. A plain fabric is best for the background squares so the colorful hearts are really pronounced.

Assemble all your scraps and decide which combinations work well together. Then enlarge the heart templates (you will need a small and a large heart for each square) on page 90 on a photocopier to appropriate sizes, or transfer them onto paper (see page 11). Using these templates, cut out the hearts. Cut the squares according to the size of pillow you require. As a guide, I found that 6-inch squares were an ideal size, but you could make smaller or larger versions of this pillow, depending on your individual requirements, or simply increase or reduce the number of squares. You may also find it useful to cut out a paper template for the squares. It is really surprising how quickly squares can become distorted when you start to use fabric pieces as templates.

Pin a small heart over a larger one. Then use three strands of colored embroidery thread and a bold overstated ladder stitch (see page 19) to secure the hearts together. Sew tiny beads over the surface of the inner heart. When you are happy with the appliqué effect, pin the hearts centrally over each linen square and sew them carefully in place, using the zigzag stitch on your sewing machine.

Choose a coordinating fabric to back the pillow and cut it out, taking into account your preferred method of closing (see pages 10-11). Sew a gauze or muslin casing for the form (see page 15) and insert it in the pillow cover. As a final embellishment, sew tiny tassels around the edges of the pillow.

Left Appliqué hearts are stitched with colored embroidery thread and tiny beads for decorative effect. Use buttons or sequins if you prefer, and look out for strands of costume jewelry in thrift stores that are often sold for next to nothing.

Right The finished pillow is composed from a variety of fabric scraps, combined to create a unique decoration. I used a natural linen, but cheaper canvas or cotton fabric would be just as effective.

Daisy-shaped cushion

Shaped cushions can make a plain chair look interesting and, provided you are careful when cutting the template, even a complicated shape such as this daisy can be stitched without a problem. See pages 14-15 for information on making shaped pillows.

Use a plate as a guide to make the paper template for the front of the cushion, and then cut out a circle of fabric. Cut the template in half, separate the two by 2 inches, and secure with adhesive tape. Use this new shape to cut out the back of the cushion. Cut the resulting fabric piece in half, and then baste the seam where the zipper is inserted and sew the remainder of the seam closed. Lay the zipper wrong side up along the basting stitches, and sew in place using the zipper foot. Undo the basting and open the zipper.

For the petal templates, see page 15. Cut out the template and use it to cut enough petals, from a double thickness of fabric (folded with right sides facing), to go around the flower. Sew an even allowance around the curved part of each petal and notch the curves using a sharp pair of scissors to ease turning. Turn through and press the seams.

Place the petals around the cushion front with right sides facing. The base of the petals should touch slightly where the stitching line is to be and the raw edges will overhang slightly. Move the petals around until they are placed correctly and stitch in place.

Cut simple flower shapes from linen fabric, backed with fusible web, and attach to the cushion front with a warm iron. Also on the front of the cushion and using the sewing machine, sew coils of stitches by dropping the feeder teeth and turning the fabric under the sewing foot as you work.

Sew the front and back parts of the cushion together, with right sides facing and raw edges even, and following the previous line of stitches. Turn to the right sides, press, and fill with a piece of thin foam cut to the same size.

Above Draw around a plate and a glass to make outlines for the paper templates.

Right Fill the daisy cover with a piece of foam cut to size, so it lies flat on the chair seat.

Appliqué peapod

The checked and gingham fabrics used to make up the front of this pillow combine to give a strong country feel. When selecting your fabrics (including the appliqué scraps), make sure they are compatible for washing together and that the colors do not run. The fringed canvas adds to the country feel, but if you prefer a neater edge turn the edges of this fabric under. An embroidered ladder stitch (see page 19) could be sewn around the canvas panel for an alternative look (see the stenciled pig on page 80, for example).

Sew together four squares of patterned fabric to make up the top of the pillow cover. Make this to the required size of the pillow, plus 1 inch all around for the seam allowance. Sew the pieces together and press the seams open at the back. Cut a plain piece of canvas or cotton fabric to make up the back of the pillow, taking into account your preferred method of closing (see pages 12-13). Finally, cut a piece of canvas to fit over the center of the pillow and fringe around the edges by teasing the threads away with your fingers.

To make the appliqué vegetables, assemble scraps of fabric and cut them roughly to size, using the peapod or carrot outlines on page 93 as a guide (if necessary, enlarge them on a photocopier to an appropriate size). Remember to include a seam allowance around each piece for turning under (see page 21). Juggle the scraps of fabric around until you are satisfied with the arrangement, and then pin them in place. Sew the appliqué pieces onto the canvas using tiny ladder stitches (see page 19). Then twist a 4 inch piece of cord to resemble the peapod stalk (see the photograph opposite), and pin this onto the canvas. Secure the cord using tiny overstitches.

When the appliqué is complete, pin and then sew the canvas square onto the front of the pillow cover, keeping the stitching line close to the fringed edge.

Sew the front and back parts of the pillow together, with right sides facing and raw edges even. Turn to the right side, press the seams, and insert an appropriate pillow form (see page 15).

Left Assemble small pieces of fabric and pin these onto the canvas. Use orange scraps for a carrot and green scraps for a peapod.

Right Coordinating country fabrics make up the main part of the pillow, and the appliqué panel is sewn over these.

Decorated linen squares

Nine squares stitched together make a generously-sized pillow, but if you would prefer to make a small pillow, reduce the number of squares. Cut them from two different fabrics to achieve the strong checkerboard effect shown here. The crown motif will be more prominent if it is stitched over a plain fabric.

Decide on the size of your pillow and divide the length of one side by three to determine the size of each patchwork square. Add ½ inch seam allowances on each side, and cut out a paper template using these measurements. Use the template to cut out the fabric squares. Sew the squares together using the sewing machine, maintaining even ½ inch seam allowances. Press the seams open on the reverse with a warm iron as you progress.

To make the gold crowns, fuse a strip of fusible web onto the reverse of a piece of gold fabric. Enlarge the crown template on page 91 on a photocopier to an appropriate size or transfer it onto paper (see page 11). Pin the template onto the right side of the gold fabric, draw around the shape, and cut out. Repeat until enough crowns are cut to correspond with the number of plain squares.

Lightly mark the center of each square with tailor's chalk. Remove the backing paper from the reverse of each crown to reveal the sticky underside. Then position each one centrally over the plain squares, using the chalk marks as a guide, and iron in place. Use gold thread and tiny overstitches to sew gold braid around the edge of each crown.

Cut the fabric pieces for the back of the pillow, taking into account your preferred method of closing (see pages 12-13). Sew the front and back parts of the pillow together, with right sides facing and raw edges even. Turn to the right side, press the seams, and insert an appropriate pillow form (see page 15).

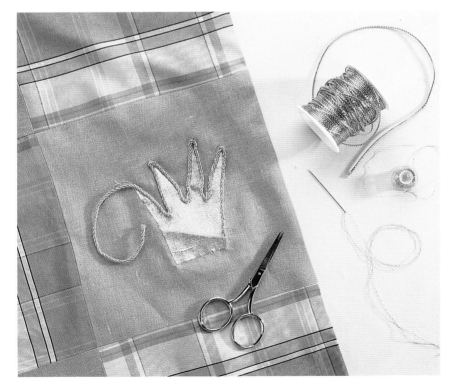

Left Sew gold cord around the edges of the crowns using a metallic thread.

Right Sew plain fabric squares alongside patterned ones to create the checkerboard effect.

Fun with fabric

Sew wonderful fringes and braids onto your existing pillow covers, or use them to add character to new ones. Pile lots of pillows together to make a welcoming stack to fall into, or display a single cover on a favorite chair - whatever you choose, these designs will bring charm to any room.

Deckle-edged pillow

The eye-catching edging on this pillow is simply made from remnants of fabric. Once the zigzags are stitched and turned right side out, they are then sewn inside the front and back parts of the pillow. When the pillow is turned right sides out, the deckle-edging is revealed.

Cut the fabric pieces for the front and back of the pillow, taking into account your preferred method of closing (see pages 12-13). The damask fabric that was used here tends to fray, so either use pinking shears to cut the fabric or stitch around all the raw edges using a zigzag stitch on the sewing machine.

For the deckle-edging, cut four strips of fabric, each 4-inches wide and long enough to stretch along each side of the pillow. Fold each one in half across the length, right sides facing, and press. Enlarge the deckle-edged template on page 91 on a photocopier to an appropriate size (my pillow is 16 inches square and each point is 2-inches wide at its base), or transfer it onto paper (see page 11). Pin the template over the strips of fabric, pointed ends toward the folds, and draw around the outlines using a piece of tailor's chalk. As each set of zigzags is drawn onto the fabric, unpin the template and move it along the strip. Match the chalk lines each time and then repin the template.

Sew the zigzags, using the chalk lines as a stitching guide. At each point of the zigzag, make sure the needle of the sewing machine is down through the thickness of fabric and then raise the foot. Turn the fabric by hand and then lower the foot to progress the line of stitching. Cut away the excess fabric and snip into the corners using a sharp pair of scissors. Finally, turn each zigzag to the right side and press the line of trimming.

Sandwich the deckle-edged trim between the front and back of the pillow, with right sides facing and raw edges aligned. Pin, then baste along each side and machine-stitch in place. Turn right sides out and tug each zigzag gently to shape, then press and insert an appropriate pillow form (see page 15).

Right Red damask with orange linen deckle-edging makes an eye-catching combination.

Woven ribbons

Choose an assortment of colorful ribbons to coordinate with your existing furnishings, or select ribbons that simply catch your eye. To make sure the colors work well together, and before you buy the ribbons, it is a good idea to pull a short length from each one and lay them next to each other. It can be very effective mixing textures as well as patterns and colors, so select velvet and satin ribbons. Different widths of ribbon will also look good.

The ribbon weave is featured on the front of the pillow only, so make this first. Cut a rectangle from a piece of mediumweight or heavyweight fusible interfacing to the size of your pillow, plus 1 inch all around for turning. This material can be purchased from fabric departments or special sewing stores and is usually sold by the yard; avoid lightweight interfacing, as this will be too flimsy.

Lay the interfacing on a flat surface with the textured (adhesive) side uppermost. Cut your ribbons to the size of the interfacing, remembering that if you are making a rectangular pillow you will need to cut two different lengths of ribbon. Pin the horizontal ribbons in place using pins at either end to secure. Butt the ribbons up closely against each other, as this will help the final appearance of the weaving. Once all the horizontal ribbons are in place, start to weave the vertical ones.

To start this, pin the first ribbon at the top left or right corner and weave it between the horizontal ones. Pin at the opposite end. Continue until all the spaces are filled with ribbon and you are satisfied with the overall look. Turn the woven fabric over onto an ironing board, and press to fuse the ribbon. Remove the pins.

Choose and cut a rich velvet, brocade or damask backing fabric, taking into account your preferred method of closing (see pages 12-13). Sew the front and back parts of the pillow together, with right sides facing and raw edges even. Turn right sides out and insert an appropriate pillow form (see page 15).

Left Back the ribbon pillow with a rich, heavy cotton velvet.

Right Remnants of all kinds of ribbon can be used to make this beautiful pillow.

Damask piped squab

Cushions that are made to fit a chair perfectly make a seat truly comfortable. This seat cushion is filled with foam, rather than conventional hollow fibers or feathers, for a cushion that will hold its shape and provide most comfort.

Cut a paper pattern for the seat cushion (see page 14). Pin the template onto a double thickness of fabric (right sides facing) and cut out the top and bottom pieces for the cushion. Prepare the corded piping from strips of bias fabric (see page 17). You will need enough piping to go around both the top and bottom of the cushion, plus 2 inches on each length for joining.

For the welt, and using the size measurements from the template (not the chair), cut out four side sections, each 3 inches wide plus ⅝ inch each end for seams. Pin the piping to the top and bottom pieces, keeping raw edges together and right sides facing. Keep the piping joins to the back of the cushion and snip the piping to turn each corner. Sew in place using the zipper foot of the sewing machine.

Sew four long ties. As a guide for the length of each one, twist a cloth tape measure around one of the chair's legs. Cut 2-inch-wide strips from the fabric for each tie, and sew across the long side and one short side, trapping a piece of string inside the tie. Pull the end of the string to turn the tie to the right side, cut off the string, and sew the ends closed. Press each tie and fold in half. Then pin each fold against the raw edges on the base of the fabric at each corner and with the loose ends facing the center of the cushion. Secure with a couple of stitches and remove the pins.

Pin the edges of the welt to the edges of the cushion, top and bottom, keeping the right sides to the inside. Align the seams at the four corners. Sew, following the stitching line made when inserting the corded piping. Leave a gap for turning; this should also be large enough to place the foam inside. Trim all the seams. Turn right sides out, insert one or two layers of foam (depending on their thickness, see page 15), and stitch the opening closed.

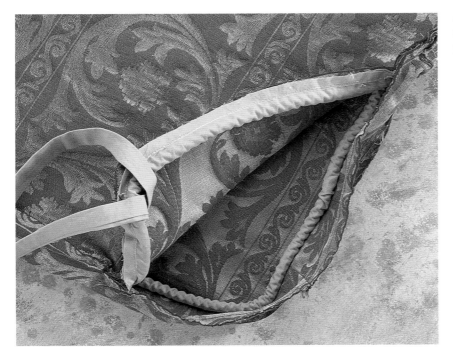

Left Leave a small gap open at the back of the cover, large enough to slide the piece of foam inside.

Right Ties not only look good, but they keep the cushion in place as well: make them extra long so that they wind down the chair legs a little.

Ohio star patchwork

This style of patchwork is made up of small pieces of interlocking fabric that fit together like a jigsaw. The star design is a traditional one, but you could make up your own patterns by marking your design onto graph paper and then cutting out the pieces. Look at quilts in museums, magazines, or books for your inspiration.

Depending on whether you want one star on the face of your pillow or the four as featured here, enlarge the star motif template on page 94 on a photocopier to an appropriate size. Then transfer the motif onto graph paper (see page 11). Use a sharp pencil and a ruler to draw the star on the graph paper, and then cut out each shape separately. You may wish to mark each shape to indicate which pieces join together (see page 22). Select your fabrics carefully. They should all be a similar weight and the colors should be colorfast; if in doubt, wash the fabrics before sewing. Avoid fabrics that may shrink.

Pin the paper templates onto the wrong side of the fabric and cut out each piece, adding a narrow margin around the edges for turning. Fold the allowance over the paper and baste these in place. Make up all the fabric pieces in this way (see page 22).

To make up the patchwork, place two adjoining pieces together, right sides facing, and use tiny stitches to sew together (the stitch should be barely visible on the right side). Continue stitching in this way, slowly building up the star pattern. Remove the basting threads, press, remove the paper templates, and then baste along the sides of the square to hold the allowances in place.

Sew three more stars in this way and then stitch them all together. Choose and cut a backing fabric, taking into account your preferred method of closing (see pages 12-13). Sew the front and back parts of the pillow together, with right sides facing and raw edges even. Turn right sides out and insert an appropriate pillow form (see page 15).

Right Blue and yellow printed cotton
fabrics in different combinations make up
this traditional patchwork design.

Scented gingham pillow

This is a ruffled pillow made from a lightweight cotton gingham - avoid heavier fabrics, because the ruffles are best when very full and soft. The lace panel that decorates the front of the pillow is, in fact, a doily that is stitched onto the front of the cover. You could use an antique handkerchief, a small piece of lace, or a decorative napkin if you wished. It may be a good solution for displaying a favorite piece of lace that would otherwise be hidden in a drawer.

Cut the fabric pieces for the front and back of the pillow, taking into account the method of closing (see pages 12-13). Your piece of chosen lace will determine the size of the pillow: as a guide, measure the panel and add 2 inches all around for a border and allowances. Also cut long strips of the gingham fabric, 7½ inches wide, for the ruffled edge. In order to achieve the soft gathered look, you will need to cut and join together enough strips to go around the outside edge of the pillow twice. You may need to join several lengths to get the long piece you require, in which case stitch together the pieces with a flat seam and press seams open.

Fold the strip in half across the width, press, and then sew the strip end to end, making one continuous loop. Sew double running stitches close to the raw edges of the strip (see page 18). Pin the strip onto the four corners on the face fabric, keeping the raw edges even. There will be twice the length of strip between each pin. Start to pull the gathering threads slowly, teasing the folds gently between your fingers and evening out the ruffles. Pin and then stitch. Pin and then stitch the lace panel onto the pillow front fabric.

Cut the backing fabric, taking into account your method of closing (see pages 12-13). Sew the front and back parts together, with right sides facing and raw edges even. Turn right sides out and fill with a potpourri sachet and a pillow form (see page 15).

Left The scent of lavender diffuses through a sachet that is placed inside the pillow together with the pillow form. Use ready-prepared potpourri or, for a really wonderful fragrance, rub the dried flower heads from a bunch of freshly dried lavender.

Right A simple lace panel is stitched over the front of this ruffled pillow.

Beanbag frog

This giant frog floor cushion is inspired by a smaller variety that is much loved by my small daughter. I have used two different types of stuffing inside the frog; the feet are filled with a soft hollow fiber filling and the legs and body are filled with polystyrene stuffing pellets to make the frog more animated.

Enlarge the frog template on page 92 on a photocopier to an appropriate size or transfer it onto paper (see page 11), and follow the instructions on pages 12-13 for making shaped pillows. Cut out the paper template and pin it onto a double thickness of fabric, folded with right sides facing. I used a bright green linen for this frog cushion, but don't feel that because the cushion has a frog character it should necessarily be green.

Remove the template and pin the two pieces of fabric together. Pin at right angles to the raw edges to allow the foot on the sewing machine to stitch over them. Stitch around the frog, leaving a small seam allowance. Due to the inevitable rough handling the cushion will be subjected to (I know ours is), I advise sewing a double row of stitches around the seams for added strength. Leave a small gap for stuffing.

Snip the curves with a sharp pair of scissors, cutting almost up to the line of stitching. Turn the frog right sides out and stuff, first with the hollow fiber in the feet and then with the polystyrene pellets - but don't pack the polystyrene into the frog tightly because the frog needs to bend and move around. There's no real easy way to fill the frog with the pellets, just pour them into the upturned frog. Sew the hole closed using strong thread and stitch beads on for eyes.

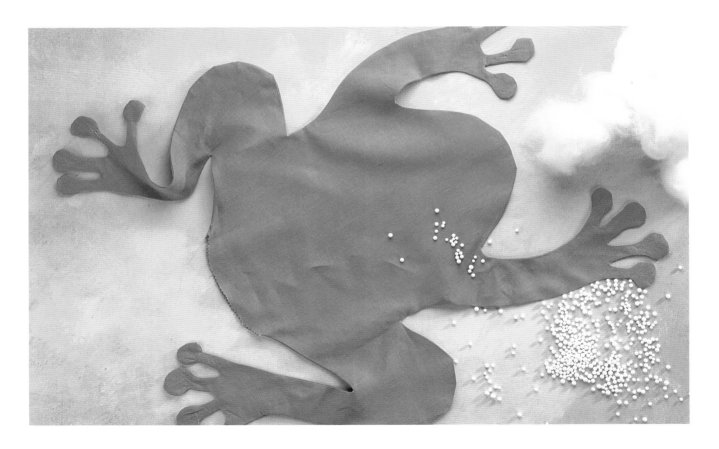

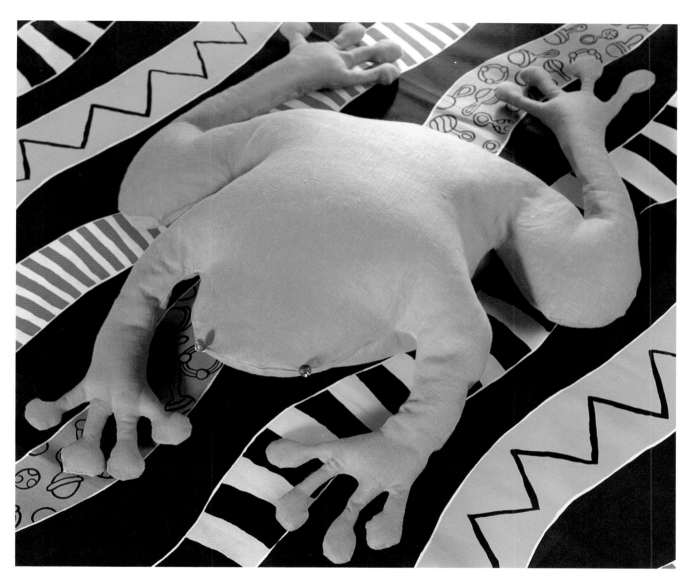

Left Fill the feet with soft hollow fiber filling to hold their shape and the body with polystyrene pellets.

Above This beanbag frog makes a really unusual floor cushion. If this frog is being made for a baby or small child, it is advisable to oversew two embroidery thread eyes on top of the frog's head, rather than using beads which may be pulled off.

Harlequin bolster

The two-tone decoration for this pillow uses a basic patchwork method. The squares are stitched together to form a flat piece of fabric, which is then rolled into a cylinder to fit around a feather bolster form.

First choose your two fabrics. They should be compatible for washing together, and preshrunk and colorfast. Then cut a 4 inch template from cardboard. Lay it onto the wrong side of one of the fabrics and use a light pencil to draw around the sides. Repeat as many times as you need squares and then cut them out. Repeat on the contrasting-color fabric. I cut out about 30 for my 20-inch-long bolster.

Stitch the squares together, maintaining an even seam allowance of ¼ inch to prevent distortion. It is a good idea to first stitch together a number of squares in pairs, then four squares, then eight and so on - always alternating the colors, of course - ending up with, say, three pieces that are then sewn together into one large piece of harlequin fabric.

The length of the patchwork will eventually need to match the length of the bolster, plus 1 inch for seams, and the width should equal the circumference of the bolster pillow form, plus 1 inch seam allowance. However, as the patchwork is displayed on the diagonal to give the characteristic harlequin pattern, you will need to make a piece of patchwork that is larger than these measurements and then trim it on the diagonal to the right size.

Above Tie the ends of the bolster in large knots or bows to secure tightly.

Left To make the triangular ties, fold four corners of a 2 inch square piece of fabric to the center and press. Place the ties over the raw edges, fold, and then sew.

Sew a rectangle of plain fabric, 10 inches wide, to either end of the patchwork. Trim to the patchwork width, and turn under the raw edges at the ends using a double hem.

To join the patchwork tube, and to ensure correct alignment of the diamonds, pin the fabric together wrapped around the pillow form and with the wrong side. Slide the form out and then stitch the seam.

Make two ties for the bolster from strips of fabric measuring 2 inches wide. Using the string method for turning (see page 48), fold each strip in half widthwise and sew along two sides. Enclose the raw ends with a triangle of folded fabric (see caption opposite, bottom) and finally bind each strip around each end of the bolster to pull the excess fabric together. Tie in a firm knot to prevent them from coming undone.

Spotted stegosaurus

This eye-catching stegosaurus uses a similar piece of zigzag edging as used for the deckle-edged pillow at the beginning of this chapter (see pages 44-45), but here it is set along the top edge of the pillow to resemble the plates on a stegosaurus's back.

Enlarge the stegosaurus template on page 91 on a photocopier to an appropriate size (my pillow is 30 inches long), or transfer it onto paper (see page 11). Cut out the template and pin it onto a double thickness of fabric, folded with the right sides facing. Cut out the fabric, remove the template, and pin the two pieces together, but leave the back unpinned for the zigzag edging. Pin at right angles to the raw edges to allow the foot on the sewing machine to stitch over them.

Stitch together a strip of contrasting fabric for the plates on the stegosaurus's back, following the method outlined for the deckle-edged pillow on page 44, but this time enlarge the template on page 91 so that each point is 3 inches wide at the base. Turn the points along the trimming to the right side and press carefully. Trim the raw edges so they are even and set this edging along the back of the shaped stegosaurus, between the front and back pieces of fabric. Keep the raw edges even and the points to the inside. Pin as before and then stitch, leaving a small, even seam allowance all around the edges. Leave a small gap at the bottom for turning out. Turn the stegosaurus right sides out, tugging the points gently to even these out.

For the colorful spots on the stegosaurus's back, iron a piece of fusible web to the reverse side of a piece of fabric in a contrasting color. Cut out small dots, remove the protective paper backing from each spot, and then place them onto the pillow. Iron in place; the adhesive is activated by heat.

Sew on buttons for the eyes, and stuff using a synthetic filling (see page 15). For babies, check the filling meets all the relevant safety checks. Sew the gap closed with strong thread.

Right Prop the pillow on a bed in a small child's bedroom or around the sides of a baby's crib.

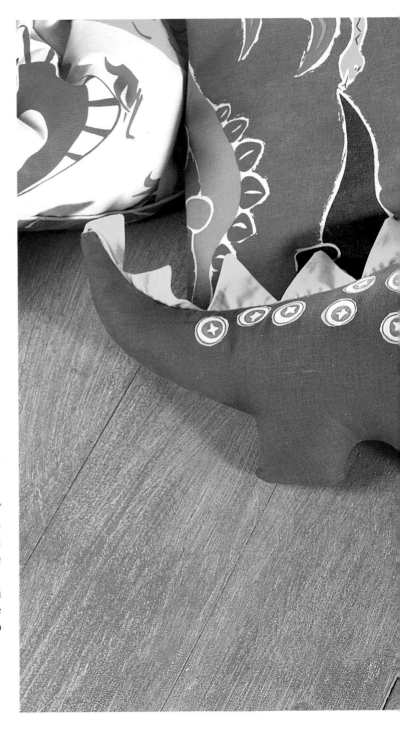

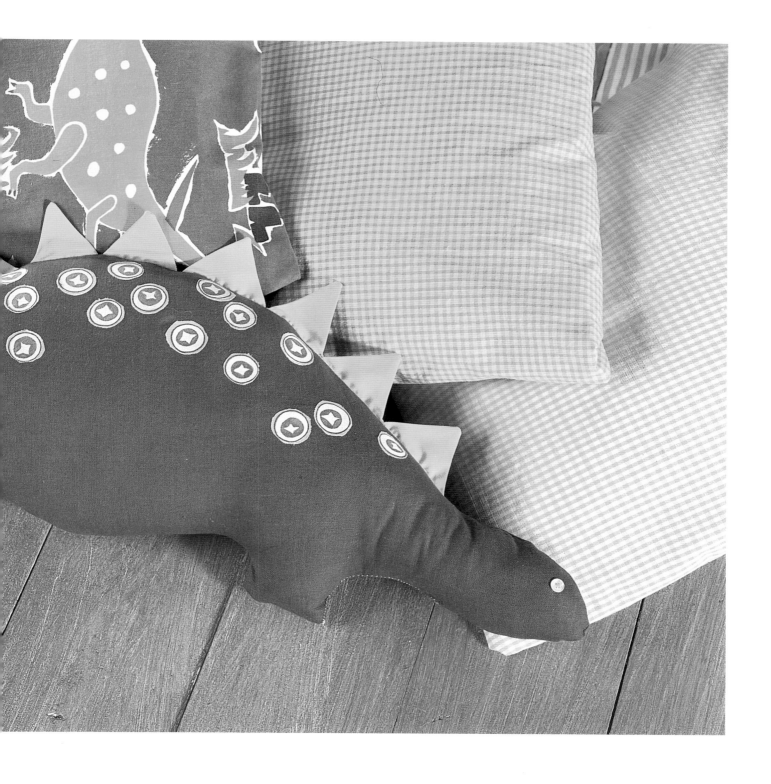

Velvet roses and leaves

This unusually-shaped pillow has a red velvet diamond stitched over a diamond-shaped, tomato red cotton cover. The lines of stitching are covered with exquisite tiny red velvet roses and green leaves for a really delightful pillow that could be propped up against the pillows on a bed or against the back of a sofa.

Cut the fabric pieces for the front and back of the pillow, taking into account your preferred method of closing (see pages 12-13). Make it diamond-shaped and use a template for cutting, following the daisy-shaped cushion instructions on page 36. Use a standard cotton duck fabric, as I have here, or, for a richer look, use damask or chintz. Then cut a diamond from the red velvet using the same paper template made for the cover, less 3 inches all around.

Pin and then sew the velvet diamond onto the center of the front face fabric, using a close zigzag stitch to seal the raw edges. Sew the front and back pieces of the pillow together, right sides facing, then turn to the right side through the back opening and gently press on the reverse side.

For the flowers, use 3-inch-wide red velvet ribbon, and for the leaves, use 2-inch-wide green velvet ribbon. Fold an 8 inch strip of red ribbon in half widthwise, velvet sides outside, and start to roll up the flower head. Bunch the ribbon occasionally to form natural-looking flowers. Fold the raw edge underneath and use long stabbing stitches to secure the rose head. Repeat, making enough roses to cover the stitching lines around the pillow.

To make the leaves, fold a 6 inch piece of the velvet ribbon in half lengthwise, right sides out, and pin. Select a close zigzag stitch on the sewing machine and thread with green cotton thread. Sew a diamond shape across the double ribbon and cut away the excess velvet. Sew across the center of these leaves to gather the velvet and create the leaf shape.

Using invisible stitches, attach the leaves and roses around the line of machine-stitching. Using the paper template, make a diamond-shaped pillow form (see page 15) and stuff it with the appropriate filling (also see page 15). Remove the form before cleaning.

Left First make lots of roses and leaves from velvet ribbons, and then sew them around the edge of the pillow.

Right Luxurious red velvet is used on the front of the pillow and decorated with velvet flowers.

Plaid rosettes pillow

Plaid fabrics are enjoying a revival at the moment and quite rightly so. These beautiful and intricate plaids can be seen on carpets, clothing, cushions and upholstery. The small rectangular pillow here is designed to support the neck, but the number of squares used can be changed to suit your requirements. Stitch nine squares to make a large floor cushion or four squares for a regular-shaped pillow.

Cut as many plaid squares (or halves) as are required for the front of the pillow, adding 1 inch all around each one for seam allowances. Attach the decorative detailing before stitching the fabric together. I have used a cross of plaid ribbon across each square, or part of square. Choose contrasting plaid ribbons, but make sure that the width of each ribbon is the same so the crosses match evenly where they meet. This is particularly important if your pillow has four or more plaid squares. Pin the lengths of ribbon in place with a single pin across each ribbon end.

Pin the squares of fabric together, with right sides facing and raw edges even. Check to see if the ribbons align, adjusting if necessary by re-pinning. Sew the squares together and press the seams open. Choose the back fabric and cut out, taking into account your preferred method of closing (see pages 12-13). Sew the front and back parts of the pillow together, with right sides facing and raw edges even. Turn right sides out, remove the pins, and press.

To make the rosettes, use 20 inches of 1½-inch-wide ribbon and make a series of tiny accordion pleats along the length. Press each fold with a warm iron to hold. As soon as four or five pleats are made, secure their base with a running stitch (see page 18). When the pleating is finished, gently pull the running stitch thread to gather the base of the folds and form the rosettes. Stitch the ends of the ribbon together, and hand-stitch a rosette to the center of each plaid square where the plaid ribbons cross. For each half rosette, halve the length of ribbon and form this into a semi-circle. Finish the pillow with covered buttons (see page 86) positioned in the center of each rosette, and insert an appropriate pillow form (see page 15).

Left When making each plaid rosette, pull the ends of the thread to draw up the pleats.

Right The rectangular pillow is designed to fit neatly into the nape of the neck to support the head.

Piped pillows

A simple row of piping adds definition to a pillow and can make a world of difference. Throughout the pages of this book you will notice several different trims, whether a double-piped trim as on the star-stamped pillow (see page 76) or gathered piping as seen on the stenciled pig pillow (see page 81). The three pillows you see here each have a different kind of piping detail, too - a multi-colored twisted cord, simple piping, and a combination of cord and piping.

Corded piping comes in several thicknesses. Generally, I use one of the thicker cords for trimming, unless the pillows are unusually small, when I would use a finer cord. Covered corded piping is generally available only in ¼ inch and 1 inch sizes, and plain cords for covering yourself are found in $^{5}/_{32}$ inch, $^{20}/_{32}$ inch and 1 inch sizes. Decorative cords can be found in an assortment of sizes.

By using decorative cords alone, you can quickly and easily embellish an existing pillow or cushion. Simply hand-sew a cord around the seam of the pillow, adding a loop at the corners for further detailing if you like. To join the ends of the decorative cord together, unravel each end slightly and then twist them back together. Firmly stitch the join to avoid unraveling; I use several overstitches to catch the silky threads which, if they unravel, will spoil the look of the cord.

For a row of single piping, see page 17 for making instructions. To bring a touch of originality to rows of single piping, you might try alternating different colors or textures of fabric. Alternatively, reverse the fabrics used on the pillows featured opposite - use brightly patterned pipings on plain pillow covers. These sort of pipings would be perfect for plain-colored pillows, as they would enliven them in a refreshing way.

An alternative trim uses both a decorative cord and a row of single piping, as shown below. Make up a pillow, inserting a contrasting piping as before. Then add the cord, making an attractive loop at each corner.

Left Hand-stitch decorative cord close to the piped edge for an unusual double trim.

Right Trim pillows with handmade piping or purchased decorative cord.

Tasseled tapestry pillow

A quick look at the price tag on any authentic tapestry pillow or cushion will leave you speechless: they do command the highest prices. However, a stroll down the racks of most upholstery fabrics will reveal some very beautiful tapestry-effect fabrics, which are positively bargains. Most of these fabrics are soft, muted colors, so a natural-colored trim would be perfectly suited to edge a pillow made from this fabric. Determine the size of your pillow and purchase the relevant amount of fabric, allowing 1 inch all around for seams. To make several tapestry pillows, select a plain canvas backing fabric so several pillows can be made from only a small amount of tapestry fabric.

To make the pillow, cut the cotton fabric to the size of the pillow, adding 1 inch all around for seam allowances. Measure the width of your trim, plus ¾ inch and 1 inch allowance for the seams, to determine the width of plain border to be left around the tapestry fabric in the center of the pillow. Measure, then cut a piece of the tapestry to fit the space. Pin the tapestry fabric centrally onto the right side of the cotton fabric. Then hand-stitch it in place, keeping the raw edges turned under as you progress. You may find it easier to press this small seam under before stitching, to make sure the allowances are even.

With right sides facing and using a complementary colored thread, sew on the trim with tiny hand-stitches (see page 16). At the corners, fold the trim neatly to form mitered edges (see below). Do not be tempted to cut the trim, as this may lead to fraying once the pillow is cleaned at a later date.

Choose the base fabric and cut out, taking into account your preferred method of closing (see pages 12-13). Sew the front and back parts of the pillow together, with right sides facing and raw edges even. Turn right sides out and press out the corners using the blunt end of a knitting needle. Insert an appropriate pillow form (see page 15).

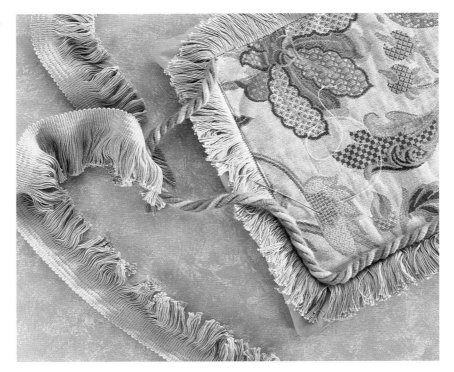

Left For a neat finish, fold the decorative trim into small mitered corners.

Right A rectangle of tapestry-effect fabric has been stitched on top of a cotton fabric, the color of which complements the tapestry. A natural-colored trim is stitched around the edge. Unusually, the trim lies flat around the face of the pillow, rather than decorating the edge in a more traditional way.

Buttoned squabs

Buttons can easily be covered in the same fabric as a pillow or cushion cover and used to provide a decorative detailing on the front of the cushion. If you are making more than one cushion, as I have done here, select different fabric for each one, but link them by color. I used three different blue and white fabrics, and finished off each one with a different arrangement of buttons - one button in the center on one cushion, and five and nine buttons grouped across the fronts of the other two.

Cut a top and bottom for the cushion cover, using the chair seat as a guide (see page 14) and remembering to include a 1 inch seam allowance all around. The cushion is stitched closed, so the front and back pieces are exactly the same. If the seat of the chair is shaped, cut a template for the fabric pieces using newspaper or brown paper. Place the paper over the seat and cut around the sides. Fold the template in half to check the symmetry and trim the paper accordingly. Remember to add the 1 inch seam allowance when cutting the front and back pieces from the fabric.

Piping gives a neat edge to these cushions. Cut a long bias strip from the same fabric to make a length of corded piping for each cushion, and then cover the piping cord (see page 17). Insert the piping into the seam of the cover between the front and back pieces, aligning all raw edges. Snip the seam allowance to turn the piping around each corner. Stitch the layers firmly together, leaving a gap along one side for turning. Turn right sides out.

For these cushions, I used a foam pad to keep the cushion flat on the chair seat and to provide the most comfort. To insert this type of filling, simply slide the cut foam into the partly-opened seam and then stitch the gap closed with neat, small overstitches, using a matching colored thread. The foam is easily cut to size using a sharp craft knife.

Cover the buttons (see page 86) and use a strong thread to sew them onto the cover, stitching through the foam as well as both layers of fabric to create the deeply buttoned look.

Left Sew the covered piping between the top and bottom pieces of the cushion cover.

Right Buttoned squabs soften a hard seat, making it more comfortable to sit on.

Freestyle pillows

Among the many designs here, you will find a mixture of various techniques to appeal to most tastes and for every room. Sew a simple pillow cover in one evening, or take your time over one of the more elaborate options.

Ribbon-edged pillow

For a unique edging detail, four lengths of wide satin ribbon are threaded through four channels of fabric stitched around the edges of this pillow and tied in a bow. A paneled fabric, as used here, is effective for this pillow, but the pillow could be made from almost any other fabric to suit your requirements. A white lace pillow, threaded with broad white ribbon, would look pretty in a bedroom, or a needlepoint pillow, threaded with velvet ribbon, would look stunning in a living room.

Cut the fabric pieces for the front and back of the pillow, taking into account your preferred method of closing (see pages 12-13). To make the channels to hold the lengths of ribbon, cut 3-inch-wide strips of a contrasting fabric to correspond with the sides of the pillow. Fold over 1 inch at each end of the four strips and press. Fold each strip in half widthwise and with right sides out to make a long, thin strip.

With the face fabric in front of you, pin the four channels along the four corresponding edges of the pillow, keeping raw edges even and right sides together. Pin at right angles to the raw edges to allow the sewing foot on the sewing machine to stitch over them. Sew the channels in place, maintaining an even seam allowance of 1 inch. Pin, then sew the base fabric over this, keeping to the same line of stitches. Trim the seams, turn the pillow to the right sides, and carefully press with a warm iron.

Cut each piece of ribbon to the same length as the channels plus 20 inches to form plump bows at each corner. Thread one end of the ribbon into a thick, round-ended needle (or compromise with a safety pin) and pass a ribbon through each channel, allowing 10 inches to hang down at either side. Once all four ribbons are threaded, tie each corner into a neat bow. Insert an appropriate pillow form (see page 15).

Above Pin the channels onto the front of the face fabric, keeping raw edges even.

Right Tie the ribbons into generous bows at each corner.

Buttoned lacy pillows

Lots of pearly buttons are used to decorate the borders of these pillows. I was lucky enough to find a whole jar of buttons in a thrift store - probably a lifetime's collection of odd assortments cut from old shirts and blouses: what a treasure. So rather than keeping these hidden away I decided to show them off and the buttons look wonderful sewn next to each other on these pretty bedroom pillows. If your collection of buttons is a little more modest, sew a single row around the lace panel, or simply make smaller pillows.

Cut the fabric pieces for the front and back of the pillow, taking into account your preferred method of closing (see pages 12-13). If you decide to make a shaped pillow, see the instructions on pages 14-15. Set aside the back pieces, as all the decoration is worked on the front.

Cut a lace panel for the front of each pillow, using the same measurements as for the pillow front, less 4 inches all around. Pin this panel onto the center of the pillow front, pinning at right angles to the raw edges to allow the foot on the sewing machine to pass over them. Then stitch around the edges using a close zigzag stitch on your sewing machine to neaten all the raw edges. Remove the pins.

Hand-stitch the buttons around the lace panel to create a deep or narrow border, depending on the number of buttons you have to hand. To create interest around the border, sew large buttons next to small ones, and pretty ones next to plain ones. Any unique or highly decorated buttons should be given prominence and sewn at the center of the borders. Cover the zigzag stitching line as you progress.

Sew the front and back parts of the pillow together, with right sides facing and raw edges even. Trim the corners and then turn right sides out. If one of the pillows is circular, notch around the seam allowance before turning to the right side to make the seam less bulky. On the back of the pillow, press the seams flat using a warm iron, and then insert an appropriate pillow form (see page 15).

Left Hand-sew a lace trim around the edges of the pillow, using small, discreet stitches.

Right A collection of buttons are far more interesting when displayed around the edges of these pretty bedroom pillows.

Star-stamped pillow

Fabric stamps are great fun to use and the character of each print varies slightly, due to the pressure applied when printing. As a result, this characteristic sets the decoration apart from manufactured prints that are unfailingly regular, and adds an attractive, hand-printed quality to the fabric.

Cut a piece of fabric for the face of your pillow; I used a pale yellow raw silk fabric to highlight the gold fabric paint. Then divide the fabric into 3-inch squares, marking each square lightly with white chalk (tailor's chalk is ideal because this has a narrow marking edge). Also mark the center of each square to provide a positioning guide for the star stamp.

Roll out a little of the fabric paint onto a flat surface; an old glazed tile, plate or piece of glass would be suitable. Cover a small roller with the paint and then transfer the paint onto the printing block. Press the block over the marked spot. Hold for a few seconds and remove the stamp to reveal each star. Do not worry if the star has lost any detailing - I think it adds to the hand-printed effect - and never put the stamp back onto the fabric, because it is difficult to realign the design.

Continue until the fabric is printed and then leave to dry. You may need to set the paint with an iron, so check the paint information.

Cut the base fabric, taking into account your preferred method of closing (see pages 12-13). For a professional finish, insert a double-piped edge by setting a narrow covered piping in front of a wider one and keeping the raw edges even (see page 17 for making piping). Pin, baste, and then sew both piping cords together onto the back of the pillow, snipping the piping at the corners to turn. Sew the pillow pieces together and turn the right sides out. Carefully press, using a piece of cotton fabric between the iron and the pillow cover, and then insert an appropriate pillow form (see page 15).

Left Use special fabric paints for printing onto pillow covers.

Right A double-piping trim gives a neat, crisp edge to this pillow.

Fringed and trimmed pillows

There are lots and lots of different trims that can be purchased to decorate new or existing pillows. The only limitation you may have is price, as some exquisite, handmade passementerie will require a bank loan, whereas others are decidedly more affordable. Look out for small lengths of trimmings in remnant bags at large stores. These are often greatly reduced and frequently contain a length perfectly suited for trimming a single pillow. Antique shops and occasionally thrift stores can unearth similar hidden treasures. I can never resist a rummage through the dusty old cardboard boxes hidden beneath piles of junk as occasionally I am rewarded with a selection of tattered trimmings bundled together with a thick rubber band.

Some trims need to be stitched between the front and back pillow pieces (see page 16), and are therefore really only practical when used for sewing a new pillow, unless you want to unpick the stitching from an old pillow cover to inset the trim. Even so, beware. On some old pillows, especially old tapestry cushions, it may only be the stitching lines that are holding them together. The ideal solution for an old pillow is to look for a trimming or braid that can be hand-stitched around the edge of the pillow.

Often more than one trim can be used on a pillow to add texture and interest. A twisted cord stitched around the edge of a fringed border, for example, can highlight a tapestry panel or add importance to an otherwise simple fabric. Heavy tassels also look effective when sewn at the four corners of a pillow or cushion.

Two of the pillows shown here feature fringed trimmings that are stitched in place once the pillow is sewn together (see page 16). It is often easier to do this once the pillow form is inside the pillow. The third, corded, trimming is inserted between the top and bottom parts of the pillow before sewing them together. This type of cord has a woven strip attached to the cord itself, and it is this that is pinned and then stitched between the pillow pieces (also see page 16).

Above Hand-sew the fringed trim around the edges of the pillow.

Right Use purchased trimmings to add instant flourish to a new or old pillow.

Stenciled pig pillow

Who could resist these charming pillows? The appliqué style of stitching used to sew the muslin pig panel onto the pillow perfectly suits the country fabric used to make the pillow cover.

Enlarge the pig template on page 90 on a photocopier to an appropriate size and then transfer it onto a piece of stencil card. Place the stencil on a suitable cutting surface and use a craft knife to cut out the pig (see page 23). Position the stencil over a piece of muslin lining and secure in place, using small pieces of double-sided adhesive tape on the reverse side. The muslin can be trimmed to the size of your pillow later on, but at this stage make sure that the pig is positioned centrally on the fabric and that there is sufficient fabric around the stencil to be cut to size later.

When stenciling, vary the amount of paint applied to some areas of the pig (see also page 23). For example, the larger body area can be patchy, whereas the tail and feet should be more heavily worked for definition. Let the paint dry and then set it according to the manufacturer's paint instructions.

Cut the fabric pieces for the front and back of the pillow, taking into account your preferred method of closing (see pages 12-13). Then cut back the panel sufficiently, so it sits comfortably in the center of the pillow with a 4 inch border of background fabric around it. Stitch the panel centrally onto the top of the pillow cover, using a close zigzag stitch on the sewing machine. Sew a deep ladder stitch around the panel, using three strands of embroidery thread in a complementary color (see page 19).

Make up the cover and, for interest, stitch a gathered piped trim around the pillow. To do this, make a regular piping case (see page 17), but sew it in place using a long stitch and do not hold the zipper foot too close to the cord. Then tease back the fabric casing gently over the piping cord to give it a ruched appearance. Pin the piping around the right edge of the top cover with raw edges aligned. Snip the piping at the corners to fit and stitch the cover front and back together. Finally, turn the right sides out, press, and insert an appropriate pillow form (see page 15).

Left Vary the pressure used on the stencil brush to build up a more interesting area of color.

Right I love the naive feel of this cute pig, and think that these pillows would look perfect in a child's room or nursery. Once the stencil is cut, why restrict yourself to only pillow covers? Substitute the fabric paint for latex paint and stencil a matching border around the nursery walls.

Heart-shaped pillow

Shaped pillows are no more complicated than square ones, as long as you make a template first (see pages 14-15). It is advisable to insert a zipper fastening when making shaped pillows, and to insert it into the back cover of the pillow to avoid fitting it around difficult curves (see pages 12-13).

Enlarge the heart-shaped templates on page 90 on a photocopier to an appropriate size, or transfer them onto paper (see page 11). For the front of the pillow, cut out one piece of base fabric using the larger-sized heart template. Then cut the template in half vertically down the center and prepare the back piece, inserting the zipper as for the daisy-shaped cushion on page 36.

To add decorative detailing to the front of the pillow cover, use the smaller heart template to cut out a coordinating piece of fabric. Pin the smaller heart over the larger one, maintaining an even allowance all the way around.

For a striking detailed edging, cut small rows of scalloping from several lengths of blue felt, enough to go all around the edge of the inner heart. Use a coin as a guide to make each scallop, and cut the felt using a small pair of sharp scissors. Slide the felt edging between the two hearts and pin securely, butting the felt strips against each other to avoid any gaps.

Sew around the inner heart using a close zigzag stitch and a blue toning thread. Then stitch the two main parts of the cover together with right sides facing and leaving the zipper open for turning. Turn the cover to the right sides and stitch around the edge of the inner heart, using blue thread to match the previous line of stitches. This creates a flat border around the edge of the pillow.

Finally, make a gauze or muslin pillow form using the larger template (see Making your own pillow form on page 15) and place it inside the cover.

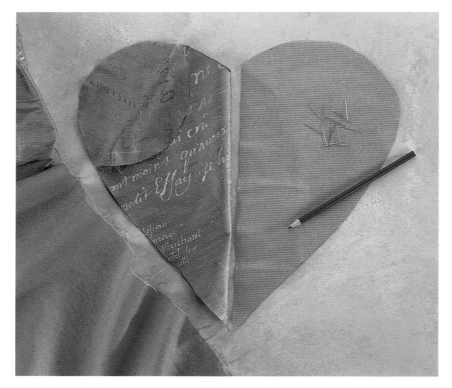

Left Use a paper template to cut the fabric to size.

Right The bright blue hand made trimming emphasizes the panel inside the heart pillow.

Aran knit pillow

Almost any pieces of material can be sewn together to make up a pillow cover, including squares cut from an old sweater. Aran or fishermen's sweaters can be bought at very little expense at thrift stores or rummage sales. Wash a woolen sweater in a very hot, soapy wash to felt the wool slightly. Sweaters marked for "hand-washing only" respond to this heavy-handed treatment perfectly, because the fibers shrink and the wool takes on a kind of attractive felted appearance. Similarly, pillows can be made from other woolen items. Scour the thrift stores for woolen blankets or shawls, for example. Likewise, a patchwork of woolen squares can be cut from scarves, sweaters or blankets, and sewn together for a checkerboard effect.

From a washed and dried sweater, cut the largest squares possible from the body of the garment; generally I find that the sleeves are too narrow to be of any real use. Inserting a zipper may be too difficult with woolen fibers and there may not be enough fabric to make an envelope closing, so stitch all sides closed after inserting the pillow form (see below).

Stitch around three-and-a-half sides, taking a regular seam allowance all around. Then select the zigzag facility on your sewing machine and, with a longish stitch, zigzag the raw edges together to prevent fraying. Turn right sides out, fill the pillow with an appropriate pillow form (see page 15), and sew the gap closed.

To add the button detailing, use a wooden toggle at both the front and back of the pillow. Knot a double strand of knitting yarn and pass this through the center of the pillow. Pull the needle through, then take a stitch and pass the needle back through to the other side. As the loop gets smaller, catch the toggle in place and pull the yarn tight. Repeat on the first side, trapping another toggle. Wind the yarn around each toggle several times before securing with three stitches and cutting off.

Left Cut the largest squares possible from the front and back of the sweater.

Right A wooden toggle is sewn onto the front and back of this pillow to complete the look.

Felt flower fastenings

I love covering buttons because you can decorate them in any number of interesting ways. These flower buttons are a real favorite and they crop up on my curtain headings, on upholstery and now on this brightly-colored pillow cover.

Stitch together a regular pillow cover, using a simple envelope closing as outlined on page 12. To create the flat border around the outside edge of the pillow, simply turn the cover to the right sides, pin across its center to prevent the fabric moving around too much, and sew a stitching line around the inside edge. Leave a regular border of approximately 2 inches all around; follow a line on the foot plate of the sewing machine as a guide. To turn the corners, check the needle is down through all the layers of fabric, lift the sewing foot, turn the fabric, and then depress the sewing foot and continue stitching.

To make the flower buttons, first determine the number of buttons you will need - this will depend on the size of your pillow, but I have made ten. Separate the two halves that make up each button and cut a corresponding number of circles from a pretty cotton fabric. Follow the manufacturer's instructions to cover the top half of the button. Then press the top half together with the bottom half to close.

Cut small flower petals from colored felt, using the template on page 90 transferred onto paper (see page 11). Snip a small slot in the center of each petal shape and push the wire stitching loop, found at the base of each button, through this. Using a strong sewing thread to attach the buttons onto the cover, sew the buttons along the stitching line made when forming the flat-edge detail. Wind the thread around the base of the button several times before finishing.

Fill the pillow with an appropriate pillow form (see page 15). If your pillow is an irregular size and you can not find a purchased form that fits, then make your own (see also page 15).

Left Cut tiny petals for the flowers from brightly-colored felt.

Right Tiny flowers sewn around the border make an eye-catching trimming on an otherwise plain pillow.

Organdy pockets

This scented pillow has real pieces of potpourri trapped beneath a layer of semi-transparent organdy fabric. The inspiration for displaying the scented fruit and flowers came from an exquisite piece of textile design created by Sara Feathers, who stitches micro-thin pieces of dried fruit and flowers into her designs. The pieces of potpourri may be crushed if the pillow is sat upon, but they will last indefinitely if the pillow is propped up among other pillows.

Cut the fabric pieces for the front and back of the pillow, taking into account your preferred method of closing (see pages 12-13). Cut a panel of organdy fabric to the same size as the front cover, less 3 inches all around. Use pinking shears if you have them to prevent fraying, otherwise turn under a tiny hem and stitch down. Pin the organdy fabric over the top part of the pillow cover, and use a ruler and tailor's chalk to divide up the pockets.

Divide each side into three equal sections, and then join the marks together horizontally and vertically to create a tic-tac-toe type of checkerboard. Pin the organdy across the center in several places to prevent the fabric slipping.

Sew along three sides of the organdy and down two vertical lines to create three long pockets that are open at their base. Tip some potpourri ingredients into each of the three pockets, making sure it slides down inside the pocket to the end of each channel. Flatten out the fabric and stitch a horizontal line across the pillow, enclosing the potpourri in a neat pocket.

Repeat this procedure twice more, until nine pockets have been created.

Sew the front and back parts of the pillow together, with right sides facing and raw edges even. Turn the right sides out and press.

To add detail to the outside seam, thread a long needle with a strand of raffia and stitch loops around the edge of the pillow, knotting each loop before moving to the next one. In this way, you will keep the loops even and uniform.

Left Slide pieces of fruit and vegetable potpourri inside the organdy pockets.

Right Complete this unusual pillow with a raffia trim.

Templates

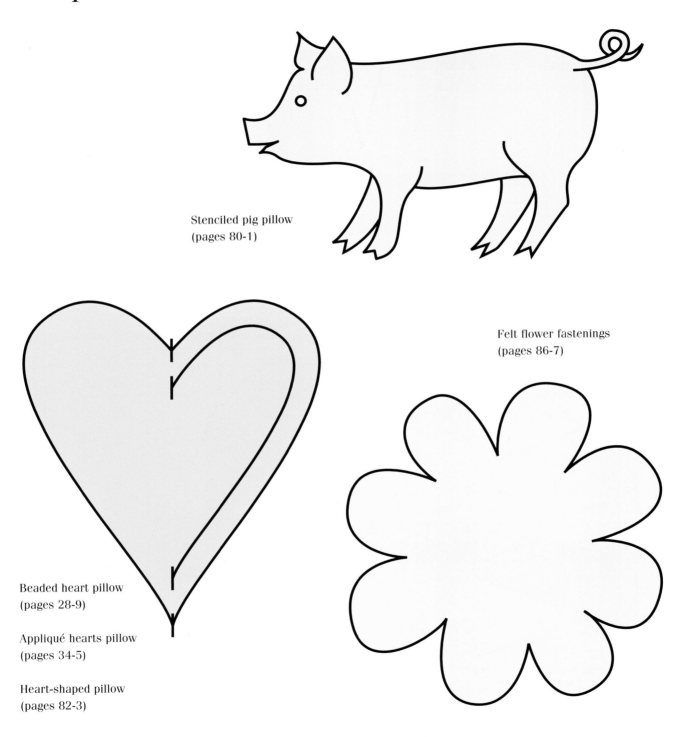

Stenciled pig pillow
(pages 80-1)

Felt flower fastenings
(pages 86-7)

Beaded heart pillow
(pages 28-9)

Appliqué hearts pillow
(pages 34-5)

Heart-shaped pillow
(pages 82-3)

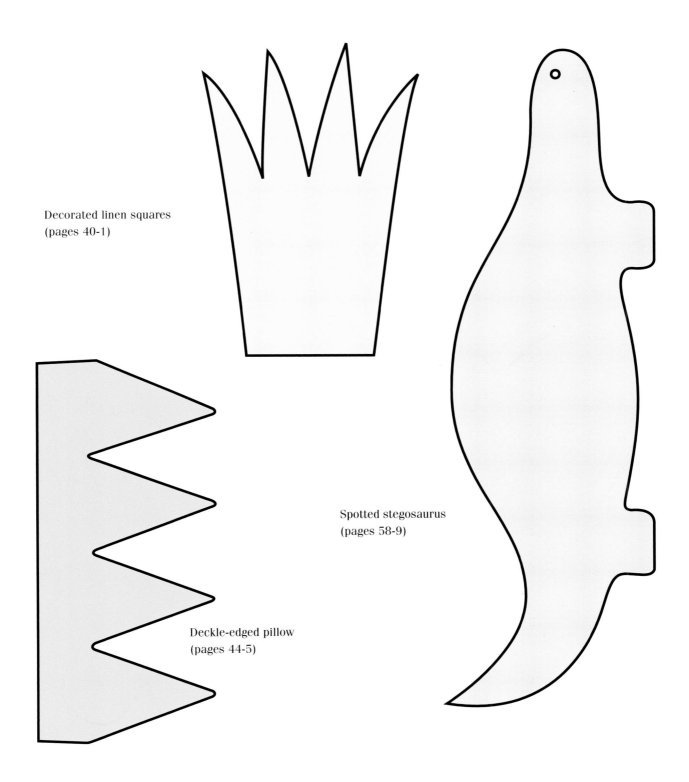

Decorated linen squares
(pages 40-1)

Deckle-edged pillow
(pages 44-5)

Spotted stegosaurus
(pages 58-9)

Beanbag frog
(pages 54-5)

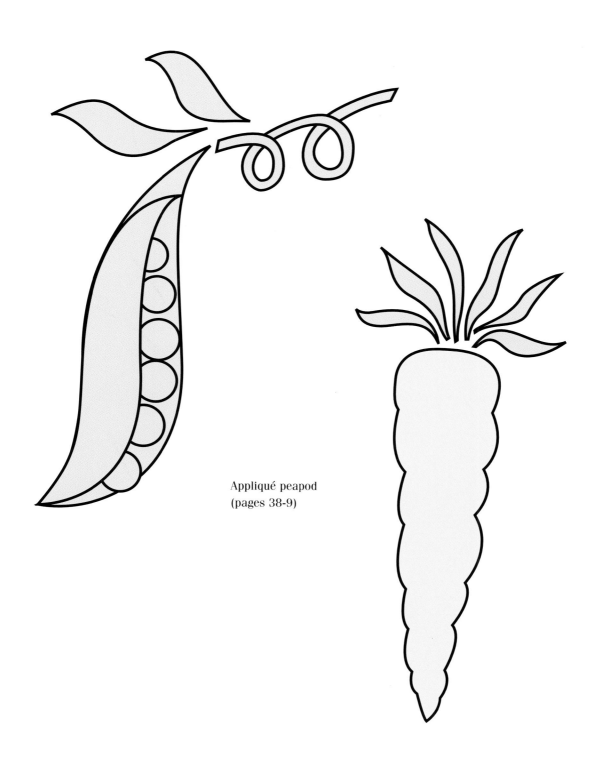

Appliqué peapod
(pages 38-9)

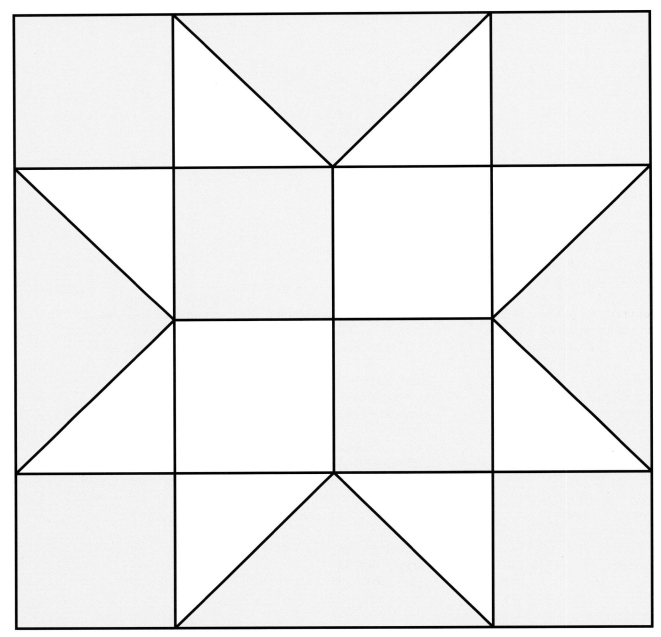

Ohio star patchwork
(pages 50-1)

Index

Acknowledgments

Props kindly loaned by:
Nice Irmas, 46 Goodge Street, London W1
Chest of Drawers, 281 Upper Street, London N1
After Noah, 121 Upper Street, London N1
Aria, 133 Upper Street, London N1

With thanks to Diane Crawford and Louise Lee for kindly allowing us to photograph in their homes.

Chair and table on front cover loaned by:
Bombay Duck, Studio 6, 14 Conlon Street, London W10